What people are saying about

Quaker Shaped Christianity

The Quaker take on the Gospels is so refreshing because it's a thread of Christianity which has, sometimes, been bashful about expressing itself. *Quaker Shaped Christianity* offers an enjoyable combination of both simplicity and depth. The first-person guidance makes the book powerful but never solipsistic, and the author's tone is exactly as I like in my theological guides: forthright and gentle. I'm convinced it will really speak to many people who are on the courtyard of the sacred but are scared of their next step.

Tobias Jones, journalist and bestselling author of books including *A Place of Refuge* and *Utopian Dreams*

This is a brave and challenging book, written in a spirit of tireless enquiry. Mark's thought process is fascinating and his conclusions are startlingly original. I thoroughly recommend *Quaker Shaped Christianity*. It is a rich, surprising, stimulating read.

Geoffrey Durham, author of *What Do Quakers Believe?*, *Being a Quaker* and *The Spirit of the Quakers*

This is an original and courageous book. Whether rehabilitating sin-talk or confronting the reality of suffering, Mark Russ does not shy away from the challenging faith questions of our time. Though the author's theological expertise is impressive, for me it is his personal faith story, and his passion for Jesus as his guiding star that illumine the book.

Jennifer Kavanagh, author of *Practical Mystics*, *The World is our Cloister* etc.

This is a beautifully crafted book, breaking the silence on what Quakers believe in a personal, powerful and compelling way. Whatever your own theological language, this is a really important book that is full of crucial theological reflections and insights.

Ben Pink Dandelion, Professor of Quaker Studies at the University of Birmingham, author of *Open for Transformation*

In this slim book Mark Russ invites us to witness his journey as he encounters Jesus and the Bible. I found myself responding to Mark's chapters as a series of meditations as he sorts through aspects of Christianity that alienated him and those which drew echoes in his being. His invitation is not about converting anyone but rather to help others see the affirmation of life he has found in this complex book with its records of Jesus' life, and to appreciate the way Friends practices and theology arise from the stories recorded therein, identifying a Quaker-shaped Christianity that he can affirm experientially.

Margery Post Abbott, author of *Everyday Prophets, Quakerism: The Basics* and other books

Quaker Shaped Christianity is an important addition to two ongoing conversations – one among Quakers, about the role of Christianity in our developing tradition, and one in the wider church, about what specific traditions like the Quaker Way can offer to Christian theology in general. Mark's combination of personal experience and broad theological reading will welcome readers from a wide range of backgrounds and speak to many conditions. Highly recommended!

Rhiannon Grant, Centre for Research in Quaker Studies, author of *Telling the Truth about God* and other *Quaker Quicks* books

By taking a personal approach and weaving in intimate memoir around his sexual identity with an exploration of Quaker and

Christian theology, Mark Russ provides readers a glimpse in a practical and profound faith journey. In *Quaker Shaped Christianity* Russ invites us into personal reflection by modeling his own vulnerability and curiosity along with the conundrums he has faced as a gay person who embraces Jesus as his guiding star.

Peterson Toscano, quirky queer Quaker Bible scholar and creator of *Transfigurations — Transgressing Gender in the Bible*

This wonderfully helpful book is accessible, yet always scholarly: it is a God-shaped book, which deserves to be re-read and cherished.

Tom Shakespeare, academic, broadcaster, author of *Openings to the Infinite Ocean* and other books

Mark Russ has given us a lovely little book that is part spiritual memoir and part spiritual invitation. He warmly invites us into exploring the Bible and Jesus and their relationship to Quaker faith and its practice. I found it enlightening. I'm certain you will, too.

J. Brent Bill, author of *Hope and Witness in Dangerous Times*, *Holy Silence: The Gift of Quaker Spirituality* and other books

Quaker Quicks
Quaker Shaped Christianity

How the Jesus story and the
Quaker way fit together

Quaker Quicks

Quaker Shaped Christianity

How the Jesus story and the
Quaker way fit together

Mark Russ

CHRISTIAN ALTERNATIVE
BOOKS

Winchester, UK
Washington, USA

JOHN HUNT PUBLISHING

First published by Christian Alternative Books, 2022
Christian Alternative Books is an imprint of John Hunt Publishing Ltd.,
No. 3 East St., Alresford, Hampshire SO24 9EE, UK
office@jhpbooks.com
www.johnhuntpublishing.com
www.christian-alternative.com

For distributor details and how to order please visit the 'Ordering' section on our website.

ISBN: 978 1 80341 054 8
978 1 80341 055 5 (ebook)
Library of Congress Control Number: 2021945742

A CIP catalogue record for this book is available from the British Library.

Design: Matthew Greenfield

UK: Printed and bound by CPI Group (UK) Ltd, Croydon, CR0 4YY
Printed in North America by CPI GPS partners

We operate a distinctive and ethical publishing philosophy in
all areas of our business, from our global network of authors to
production and worldwide distribution.

Contents

Theology is... imagination for the kingdom of God in the world, and for the world in God's kingdom. **Jürgen Moltmann**

Acknowledgements

This book is dedicated to all my theological mentors, all those people who have encouraged me in my reading, thinking and writing, as I've tried to make sense of the presence of God in my life. I give thanks for the work of Jürgen Moltmann, whose books taught me that theology can be beautiful, inspiring, and readable. His fingerprints can be found on most of the pages of this book. I am particularly grateful to Rhiannon Grant, Deborah Shaw and Ben Wood for their wisdom and valuable feedback on the first draft of this book, to Lloyd Lee Wilson for his insightful critique, and to my husband, Adrian, for his proofreading skills. The encouragement of Michael Burdett both during and after my MA studies has been invaluable. My dissertation produced under his supervision laid the groundwork for this book. Above all, I am thankful for my parents Claire and Brian Russ. Although I suspect they wouldn't think of it in these terms, through the loving home they gave me, and the self-love they instilled in me, they grounded me in the love of God, the love that has become the bedrock of my theology.

Introduction

My Quaker-shaped Christianity

The word "Quaker" first caught my attention in a history class at the age of 17, whilst learning about the English Civil War. I remember the teacher saying that Quakers caused a lot of trouble, particularly as they didn't believe the Bible was the last word. As a teenager struggling with big questions about faith, and seeing the Bible as a rather large stumbling block, that was enough to grab my attention. Some people discover Quakers when searching for a place of quiet reflection. Others stumble across Quaker vloggers on YouTube or meet Quakers at a peace vigil. For people who have these brief encounters with Quakers and experience a spark of connection, like I did in that history class, the next question is "What is Quakerism?"

Quakerism is a largely Christian religious movement that began in seventeenth-century England, and which can now be found all over the world. Although the number of Quakers globally is small compared to other religious groups, there's still a surprising amount of variety within Quakerism. Being a Quaker in Bolivia can look very different from being a Quaker in New Zealand or in Kenya. Quakers in Britain, where I live, can be described as "liberal" Quakers, and this is the sort of Quakerism I write about in this book. One of the characteristics of liberal Quakerism is theological diversity. Quakers in Britain don't all believe the same things, or use the same words to describe our spiritual experience. That means "What is Quakerism?" is an increasingly difficult question for Quakers in Britain to answer. It's perhaps easier to say how Quakerism isn't like other forms of Christianity: no hymns, no bread and wine, no priest at the front. Or maybe it's easier to focus on what Quakers do: silent worship and anti-war demonstrations.

The real difficulty lies in saying what Quakers believe. Now that I'm a Quaker, I find myself unable to speak for all Quakers. We tend to shy away from discussing our beliefs, finding unity in a shared silence. Unfortunately, this silence makes it even more difficult for people to find out what Quakerism is, and stops Quakers from knowing one another better. At worst, this silence doesn't really unite us at all. It becomes the rug we sweep our differences under. The silence prevents us from learning one another's religious language, to the point where we can no longer understand or communicate with one another.

This book is an attempt to break the silence and bring some of our differences out into the open. It offers a very specific response to the question "What is Quakerism?" I don't provide a broad overview of the Quaker landscape, or an answer that captures the variety of global Quakerism. I don't attempt to speak for all Friends (as Quakers refer to themselves). Instead, I offer my own individual perspective, *my* Quaker-shaped Christianity. This Christianity is shaped by who I am, a body in a particular time and place. I'm a white, English, cis, non-disabled gay man, a millennial from a middle-class, relatively affluent upbringing – all factors that mold my religious experience and outlook. My explorations of Quakerism and Christianity, the books I've read, the conversations I've had, the relationships I've formed – all these things feed into the Quaker-shaped Christianity I hold today. So in order for the rest of this book to make sense, I need to tell you my faith story.

About me

I grew up in a non-religious family in the East Midlands of England. We were culturally Christian in that we celebrated Christmas. As a musician my Decembers were filled with carol concerts, and I still love to belt out "O come all ye faithful," but church-going wasn't something we did. Sundays were for relaxing in front of the TV. My dad had been forced to attend church alone as a teenager by my grandparents, because it had been "good enough for them" when they were his age. This led him to see Christianity, and all religious belief, as hypocritical nonsense. As a baby, I was baptized into the Church of England, but this was to keep my religious maternal Grandma happy. Having soaked up this mixture of ambivalence and animosity to religion at home, my own opposition to Christianity was formed by my time as a Cub Scout. I vividly remember being told off for not knowing the Lord's Prayer by heart, which, as someone who didn't know what the Lord's Prayer even was, I found bewildering! My membership of the Scouts ended abruptly after attending a Christmas "party." Being a shy, tubby eight-year-old with few friends made this awkward enough, but what sticks in my mind to this day was having to sit through a long, incomprehensible sermon from an Anglican priest, and then being given one small piece of cake when I'd been expecting at least a sandwich or two. If this was a Christian idea of a party, I wasn't interested. Religion was mystifying and boring. In my early teens this confusion transformed into moral outrage. At 14, whilst playing the organ at my uncle's Anglican church, I was invited to take bread and wine communion on the grounds that I was baptized. I was appalled that something which happened to me as a baby, which I didn't choose or remember, gave me special access to something that others were denied. The Christians I encountered at school fueled my opposition to religion, with their open, self-righteous homophobia. By 16 I was a fervent atheist, seeing Christianity as irrelevant, hypocritical, and superstitious.

At 17 I began, slowly, to come out as gay. I felt that continuing to keep my sexuality a secret would damage something deep inside me. My coming out was accompanied by a number of intense spiritual experiences. Accepting my sexuality allowed me to accept my spirituality. I didn't know what to make of these experiences, and I needed a space to explore. I was in no doubt that being gay was absolutely fine, and so knew Christianity wasn't an option for me. After discovering Quakers in a history class, and then borrowing some Quaker books from the mother of a close friend, I discovered a religious group who didn't require me to believe anything in order to go. So at 17 I experienced my first Quaker meeting for worship.

In Quakerism I found the spaciousness I was looking for. Because Quakers are opposed to creeds (statements of belief), and are encouraged to speak about faith in an authentic way, I could experiment with words that best described my experience. I quickly found "God" to be a good name for the expansive love I felt in the silence of Quaker worship. I was able to talk about God without committing to any particular beliefs about Jesus, or labeling myself as a Christian. Over the years, my fascination with Jesus and the Christian tradition grew. There was something captivating about Jesus. I began to meet other Christians, including queer ones, who weren't like the Christians I'd known growing up. They weren't judgmental or trying to save me from an eternity in hell. The hypocrisy, irrelevance and discrimination I'd encountered as a teenager wasn't the last word on Christianity.

Because Quakers in Britain are a small community, and one that doesn't spend much time discussing theology, I generally went outside Quakerism for my religious education. To make sense of Jesus I read books, went on courses and retreats, and attended a Christian festival called Greenbelt. I met my non-Quaker husband through a LGBT+ Christian network. I found that, because of the negative experiences I'd had of Christianity growing up, I needed to unpick a number of theological knots before I could read the Bible. Seeing Christians use the Bible to bolster their homophobia, I couldn't dive straight in. I had to read lots of books about the Bible first. As I got deeper into my explorations, more things clicked into place. I began to see meaning in the more mysterious claims about Jesus. I became convinced that Jesus rose from the dead – whilst still understanding it as intensely mysterious.

This journey has led me to call myself a Quaker-shaped Christian. I now see Jesus as the key to my experience: the Jesus story makes sense of my life, and I see the world through the Jesus story. Christian writer G. K. Chesterton said that when a key fits a complicated lock, you know it's the right key. For him, the complexity of Christianity matches and makes sense of the complexity of the world. This metaphor resonates with me. The Jesus story makes sense of my experience both emotionally and intellectually. It gives me answers to my questions. It has a depth and breadth that seems to contain everything, whilst never feeling restrictive. It's a story that contains hope, justice, love and freedom, history, politics and spirituality, and addresses the very worst and the very best in us.

I've found being a Quaker-shaped Christian requires a "patchwork" approach to my religious life. Being a Christian, I find it important to spend time with others for whom Jesus is central. I'm part of a house group with Christians from other churches, occasionally visit cathedrals, go to Franciscan monasteries on retreats, and follow lots of Christian theologians on Twitter. But I'm also Quaker-shaped. I "speak Quaker." I feel at home in Quaker settings. I know what it feels like to be called to speak in Quaker worship. I'm inspired by the insights of my Quaker forebears, I value the progressive nature of the contemporary Quaker community in Britain, and I'm thankful for the many wonderful Quakers who have come into my life. I couldn't have become a Christian in any other church.

About this book

In making this book very personal, I hope to cut through the hesitancy Quakers often experience in describing Quakerism. But this book's strength is also its weakness. Taking a personal approach means that this book has its limitations. When I talk about Quakerism and Quakers in this book, I'm talking about Quakerism as it is practiced in Britain. Without ignoring or erasing all the other sorts of Quakerism in the world, for the sake of simplicity I will use "Quaker" to refer only to Quakers in Britain for the rest of this book.

In talking of Quaker-shaped Christianity, I'm not saying that being Christian is the only way to be a Quaker. Neither am I saying that you must be a Quaker to be a "real" Christian. There are many ways to be Christian, to be Quaker, and to be a Quaker-shaped Christian. There is no "pure" Quakerism or "pure" Christianity. If there's one thing Christians have in common, it's arguing about what it means to be a Christian! This book is a contribution to that argument, not an attempt to end it. I don't want to imply that Quaker-shaped Christianity is unique. Although there may be some differences, there are many more overlaps and commonalities with other Christian traditions. At the same time, while this account of Christianity is one among many, it doesn't mean I think that all accounts of Christianity or Quakerism are of equal value! There are interpretations of Christianity and Quakerism that are problematic and harmful. I hope to offer a Quaker-shaped Christianity that is useful, coherent, and convincing. Although this is *my* Quaker-shaped Christianity, that doesn't mean I feel possessive about it. I definitely want to share it. I hope that others may recognize their own experience in mine, or that some might be inspired to explore Quaker-shaped Christianity for themselves.

This book is fed by conversations with Quakers and Christians from the last twenty years. I've often had to explain my beliefs to Quakers who find Christianity strange, unpalatable or pure nonsense. Each chapter reflects a conversation I've needed to revisit again and again. As such, there'll be many aspects of Christianity and Quakerism that I don't cover. The Jesus story is a big story that has been argued over for centuries. There are bound to be things missing, perhaps things you find particularly important. I can only apologize. This is also probably not the best book for those completely new to Quakerism and Christianity. In this book I assume at least a passing familiarity with both. Thankfully there are many other books available that make up for what is missing here.

With all of those caveats, I hope this book will be useful to a range of people, including: people who are curious about how Christianity and Quakerism can go together; people who have had bad experiences of other Churches, and are wondering how a Quaker form of Christianity might be different; and Christians who want to understand how a Quaker-shaped Christianity is similar and different from their own tradition.

In Chapter 1, I explain my approach to the Jesus story that is found in the Bible. The last three centuries have seen a search for the "historical Jesus," trying to get behind the writers of the New Testament to find the "real" Jesus. In this chapter I explain why this search is a dead end. As I see it, there is no distinction between the Jesus of history and the Christ of faith. The only Jesus we have access to is the Jesus who the biblical authors name the Christ. This means that, if we want to engage with Jesus, we also need to engage with the bigger story he's a part of. This means reading the Bible, not uncritically or literally, but treating it as a conversation partner. In Chapter 2, I respond to the challenge of universalism, the belief that all religious paths lead to God, and are equally true. In a Quaker community where not everyone is a Christian, why am I focusing on Christianity at all? Why choose one particular story, when so many other stories are available? Quakers are known for their commitment to peace, and in a multi-faith world my insistence on a specifically Christian approach might appear exclusive and divisive. In this chapter I explain my difficulties with universalism, and why a Quakerism that is specifically Christian can still be a way of inclusivity and peace. In the remaining chapters, I focus on four significant events in the Jesus story. Instead of starting with Jesus' birth and working forward, I start with the end of the story – what is known as the Second Coming – and work backwards. I believe that the Jesus story can only be understood in the light of its ending, and this is reflected in the rest of the book.

In Chapter 3, I explore "the Second Coming." This part of the Jesus story has a history of being told badly. I explain how it is better understood, not as a cataclysmic event still to come, but as a process of God's "arrival" into the world. This sense of "arrival" is part of Jesus' ministry, particularly his teaching on the Kingdom of God. Quaker-shaped Christianity is a faith of desire for a Christ-shaped future, a desire that energizes us to work for a better world. We can taste the Kingdom in the present moment, but the full feast is still to come. In Chapter 4, we come to the Resurrection of Jesus. I share how I make sense of the Resurrection, specifically in what it has to say about release from the fear of death and death-dealing powers, the hope of justice for all, and freedom, both inward and outward, spiritual and material. In Chapter 5, I look at what we are liberated from – death-dealing powers and those who wield them – and how the Crucifixion exposes these powers. I explore the harmful ways sin is talked about, how sin can still be a useful word, and the political nature of the cross. The cross has an inward and outward nature, and unites the mystic and the activist. In the final chapter, I draw my reflections on Quaker-shaped Christianity together using the metaphor of the seed. I describe how the Nativity is a seed of the Jesus story, how the first Quakers spoke of the seed, and how Mary, mother of Jesus, bearer of Christ the seed, can be seen as a model of Quaker-shaped Christianity.

Most, if not all books are a communal effort. I couldn't have written this book without drawing on the ideas of others. To honor these people, I end with a section called "Notes." Here I reference all the voices that fed into the writing of this book.

This will also make it easier for you to follow up the ideas I mention, and explore them further for yourselves. All biblical quotes, unless otherwise stated, are from the *New Revised Standard Version*. Because I don't want to assume a particular level of biblical literacy, whenever I first mention a particular book of the Bible, I give its full name (e.g., 1 Corinthians). Further mentions are then abbreviated in a conventional way (e.g., 1. Cor.).

Chapter 1

The Jesus Story – Approaching the Bible

At the center of Christianity is the life of a first-century Palestinian Jew: Jesus. The information we have about him is almost entirely contained in the writings of the early Church, which collected together we call the New Testament. Because Jesus was a Jew, and Christianity began as a movement within Judaism, the New Testament continually references the stories and wisdom of the Jewish scriptures known either as the Old Testament or (as I will call them in this book) the Hebrew Bible. All of this means that if we are to learn about Jesus, who he was and why he was significant, we can't avoid the Bible.

During my first explorations of spirituality as a teenager, avoiding the Bible was exactly what I wanted to do. I was generally pro-Jesus, he seemed like a good guy, but the Bible was another matter. When I tried to read it for myself, I found it a mysterious, incomprehensible book. I'd hear Christians talk about the Bible as if it was an easy-to-read instruction manual, but there was nothing clear about it. I also saw Christians using the Bible as a weapon, against women, people of other faiths, and gay people like me. As well as being impenetrable, and a tool of hatred, the Bible was filled with wild supernatural claims. I didn't know what to make of Jesus being the son of God, performing miracles and rising from the dead. I was intrigued by Jesus, I wanted to know more about him, even follow him, but without the baggage of fundamentalism, or the "supernatural" parts of the story. I wanted Jesus without the Bible. In this chapter, I'm going to describe my attempts to find Jesus in this way, and how I ended up returning to the Bible, to the Jesus story, as a foundation stone of Quaker-shaped Christianity.

Where is the "real" Jesus?

My search for Jesus began with the stories about Jesus called the Gospels, specifically the Gospel of Mark. It's the shortest and earliest Gospel, and in its earliest form it ends with the disciples fleeing the empty tomb, so I could read it without worrying about the Resurrection. I thought that in the Gospel of Mark I could get closer to the "real" Jesus. Even then, I still approached Mark and the other New Testament writings with caution. These documents are nearly two thousand years old, and were written down years after Jesus' death. They're more concerned with making claims about Jesus than describing his life. The New Testament authors have definitely got an agenda. They make claims that bear no relation to my own experience – a Virgin birth, walking on water and people coming back from the dead. How could I get behind this dubious collection of texts to the "real" Jesus?

This is exactly the question that biblical scholars began to ask in seventeenth- and eighteenth-century Europe, in the period called the Enlightenment. They approached the Bible with suspicion, and started what has come to be known as "the Quest for the Historical Jesus." These scholars were like archaeologists, attempting to scrape away the layers of superstition and myth, and find the real human being beneath. As the Quest continued into the nineteenth century, thousands of "Lives of Jesus" were written, biographies of the "real" Jesus describing his personality, spirituality and psychology. The "real" Jesus they discovered was a moral teacher who offered a way to inward peace and a well-lived life. This Jesus represented the high point of spiritual evolution to which all humanity was gradually progressing. Towards the end of the nineteenth century, Quakers began to adopt this approach, and the influence of the Quest can still be felt in Quaker attitudes to Jesus today.

Unfortunately, there are a couple of significant problems

with the Quest. Firstly, when we try to search for the "real" Jesus in places other than the New Testament, we quickly discover that there are hardly any other sources of information about Jesus. Outside the New Testament, there isn't enough evidence to build a coherent picture of him. Once we take away everything in the New Testament that doesn't fit with modern sensibilities, the most we can say about Jesus is that he was a failed revolutionary executed by the Romans. The writers of the "Lives of Jesus" didn't want to paint such a meagre picture. Like me, they felt that there was something inspiring about Jesus that had relevance to our lives today. This leads to the second problem. Without the extra-biblical evidence to build a coherent picture of Jesus, these writers unintentionally produced images of Jesus that looked very much like themselves, like nineteenth-century European Protestants. They created Jesus in their own image. These "Lives of Jesus" were famously described as like looking into the deep dark well of history, and seeing your own face reflected back.

These problems with the Quest have led me to see that when I try to find Jesus without the Bible, there is no one there. There is no Jesus accessible to me other than the Jesus of the New Testament. If I attempt to sift out "author bias" or other aspects of the Jesus story I find unpalatable, I end up creating Jesus in my own image. If I approach the Bible hoping to find a purely human, moral teacher, I need to recognize that the authors of the New Testament are not interested in describing such a Jesus. They are not concerned with Jesus' personality or psychology. Their sole purpose is to announce him as the Messiah (the Christ) and the one that God has risen from the dead. This means I can't make a distinction between the "Jesus of history" and the "Christ of faith." To engage with Christianity means having to account for all aspects of the Jesus story. If I think Jesus is worth engaging with at all, I must allow myself to be challenged by the Jesus I meet in the New Testament. If I try to go "behind" the New Testament, I will invariably arrive at a Jesus of my own making.

There are no "added extras"

Having realized I needed to approach the New Testament as a whole, I still needed to "explain away" the difficult claims about him, like him being the Messiah. One way I could do this was to see these claims as "added extras" that aren't essential to his life and message. Again, this approach has been tried before. The writers of the "Lives of Jesus," as well as portraying Jesus as a human moral teacher, also imagined Jesus as teaching spiritual wisdom that transcended all religious traditions. What mattered to these writers was Jesus' teaching about inward spiritual experience. The historical specifics of Jesus' life, like his Judaism, were just "window dressing." He only spoke in Jewish terms because of his culture. If he had been born into another religious culture, he would have used different terms to express the same underlying spiritual message. His Jewishness could even be seen as an obstacle for Jesus to overcome. His teaching transcended his Jewishness.

This approach is a popular one with modern Quakers, to the point where we might not be able to imagine Quakerism without it. It's not uncommon to hear Quakers say there's a universal religious experience that all people share, and we give this experience various labels, depending on our culture. Our experience comes first, and the stories and ideas we use to describe this experience come second. Thinking along these lines, we might say that the first Quakers, like Margaret Fell and George Fox, spoke in Christian language purely because that reflected the culture they were living in. If they had been in an Islamic culture, they would have used symbols and language from Islam. On this view, Christianity is incidental. It becomes an "added extra." There's a core universal message that transcends the images, language and symbols of any religion.

Initially, I thought this approach gave me access to the real, universal Jesus without the challenging specifics of the Jesus story. Now, I don't think it's that simple for two reasons. The first is to do with the relationship between experience and culture. I don't think there's such a thing as a pure, universal religious experience that is untouched by language, images and culture. How do we know such an experience exists? We can't step outside ourselves, outside culture, to see if this is so. We use language, stories and images to interpret our experience, and they in turn shape the experiences we have. Our culture and our experiences are so intertwined that we can't separate them. This means that Jesus, Christianity and the language of the Bible are not "added extras" to the experience of the early Quakers. The early Quaker experience is inseparable from the Jesus story.

The second reason is particularly important. This is about how we approach Jesus the Jew. If we say that Jesus' Jewishness was incidental to his message, then we're saying that his Jewishness is dispensable. This is exactly how Christian antisemitism has operated over the centuries. In the second century, a Christian called Marcion tried to find the real Jesus separate from Judaism. To do this, Marcion literally dispensed with the Hebrew Bible, as well as everything in the New Testament he considered too Jewish. He believed that the message of love preached by Jesus had nothing to do with the "angry God of the Old Testament." This is a belief still held by many Christians today, including some Quakers, and it's a gross misrepresentation of Judaism and the Jewish scriptures. We meet God as Love in the Hebrew Bible, and we meet God as Judge in the New Testament. If we say that Jesus' Jewishness is not relevant to his message, then we are repeating an anti-Semitic trope. The biblical story describes a God who is revealed in a specific time and place. God chooses a particular people to be in relationship with (the Jews). This is why Jesus says that "salvation is from the

Jews" (John 4:22) and that he "was sent only to the lost sheep of the house of Israel" (Matthew 15:24). But Jesus also makes explicit that God's intention is to draw non-Jews (the Gentile "nations") into this relationship, that God's Temple "shall be called a house of prayer for all the nations" (Mark 11:17) and that the wall that divides insider and outsider will be broken down (Ephesians 2:14). This is such a fundamental part of the biblical "plot," that denying Jesus' Judaism makes the biblical story incomprehensible.

I have found that there is no Jesus other than the Jesus the early Church claimed was the Messiah, and the title "Messiah" is a Jewish one. There is no other Jesus than Jesus the Jew. Acknowledging this is easier than working out what it means. Historically, Christians have spent very little time thinking about Jesus the Jew. Perhaps one place for me to start is to reflect on what it means to be a Gentile, a non-Jew. What does it mean for me to be an outsider who is invited in? This is an especially important question for me, because white European men are used to seeing themselves at the center of the world. As a white European man, what does it mean to see myself as a foreigner who is invited into God's house of prayer?

Inhabiting the Jesus story

To take Jesus seriously, I needed to explore the early Church's claim that Jesus is the Messiah who God raised from the dead. I needed to engage with the New Testament and the Hebrew Bible, but there was still an obstacle in my way – biblical literalism. Did taking Jesus seriously mean I had to treat everything in the Bible as literally true? This was certainly the impression the Christians I knew as a teenager gave me. Because of the dominance of certain types of conservative Christianity in the world, many people think that literalism is the only way to read the Bible, and perhaps how the Bible has always been read. But a literal approach, the sort that gives rise to Creationism and the belief that the universe is only 6000 years old, is actually a very modern way of reading the Bible. It's a conservative reaction to the Enlightenment-inspired questioning of the Bible I spoke of earlier, and it's caused a lot of problems. There are other ways to read the Bible. Taking the Bible seriously does not mean taking it all literally.

Whether we see the Bible as either unreliable propaganda, or as a rigid, authoritarian rule book to be interpreted literally, I think we're asking the same question: "did these events happen exactly as described?" To this question the liberal answers "no," and the fundamentalist answers "yes," but this is a very modern question to be asking of a very old collection of texts. I now approach the Bible with a different set of questions, beginning with "what are the original authors trying to say about God, and about Jesus?" As someone who believes that Jesus is relevant to my life today, I can't stop there. I then need to ask "how do the insights of these authors speak to me now?" Through asking these questions I began to see the Bible as a conversation partner, and I realized that to be a Christian is to join a community of argument. The one thing that has united Christians over the centuries is the debate about what it means to be a Christian. Christianity is a millennia-long conversation about the significance of the Jesus story.

The first Quakers approached the Bible in a similar way. They took the Bible seriously, and believed it was indispensable. They also stressed that the same Spirit that inspired the biblical authors could inspire us today. In fact, they said that we could only interpret the Bible correctly through this inspiration. The Jesus they read about in the Bible was present with them as a guide, teacher and friend. By asking "what canst thou say?" they brought the biblical authors into dialogue with their own experience. Our lived experience shapes how we read the Bible, and this is how it should be. We can never reach a "pure" or "objective" reading of the Bible, because the Bible is always read by people, people who bring their own particular perspective with them whenever they read it. This only becomes a problem when one type of lived experience is privileged over another. It's important for me to bring my experience as a queer person to the Bible, and I need to be aware of other ways of reading the Bible beyond my experience. Because it's a conversation, there isn't one way to read the Bible. What about the experiences of people of color? Of disabled people? Of women? Of trans people? All this talk of storytelling is not to say that the existence of a historical Jesus is not important. Quite the opposite! If Jesus did not exist as a real figure in human history, then there is no foundation for Christianity. It also doesn't mean that every perspective is equally right. Although there are multiple ways of reading the Bible, some are more life-giving than others. This is why it's a community of argument and debate – we're working out together how to interpret the Bible in the most life-giving ways.

A particularly important part of this conversation concerns gender. Although it is often stated that the God of the Bible is not like human beings, and in many ways beyond our imagining (e.g., Exodus 33:20), God is also constantly referred to using male pronouns. This sort of language, coupled with familiar images of God as an old bearded man, creates a strong impression of God as a man. When this is combined with the idea that God is revealed in Jesus of Nazareth, a man, then it can seem as if Christianity has nothing to say to women. If God is seen as male, then this encourages men to see themselves as God. Feminist theologians have done much to critique and dismantle this image of a male God. In the Hebrew Bible, God is sometimes referred to using feminine and genderless imagery. There are ways in which Jesus challenges the gender norms of his day. I'm particularly taken with fourteenth-century English mystic Julian of Norwich's description of Jesus as Mother. There are also many women in the biblical story through whom

God is revealed. In this book I use gender-neutral pronouns for God, such as "God's" or "God's-self," and less gendered terms like "Spirit." There's not space in this book to do this subject justice, but it's important to acknowledge this vital part of the conversation, one I need to pay close attention to as a man.

As well as allowing my lived experience to shape how I read the Bible, I also need to allow the Bible to shape my lived experience. I need to allow the strangeness, the otherness of Jesus to challenge me. As well as seeing myself in conversation with the Bible, I also see the biblical story as a story I can inhabit. I allow the voices and stories of the Bible to shape my life. I can make the biblical story my own story. Christianity is a historical, story-driven faith. By that I mean Christianity isn't a collection of timeless, abstract truths. Christianity is about a God who acts in history. The Jesus story is a drama, moving from the past into the future. Christianity is a story to be entered into, a drama to act in. In the Bible, prophets receive the word of God they must speak in the form of a scroll they must eat. I find this a helpful image for studying the Bible. Rather than being an instruction manual or encyclopedia to be referenced, it's something to absorb, to digest, to have within me. Through spending a lot of time with the text, I begin to make connections and get to know its complexities. As I become familiar with its metaphors, symbols and images, they come to me when I need them. The first Quakers were soaked in the Bible. Their writings are full of different biblical texts woven together to create messages relevant to the people they were addressing. To use another metaphor, this approach to the Bible is like being a jazz musician – by absorbing the language and symbols of the Bible, we're then able to riff off them and create the music that needs to be heard today.

My journey to know Jesus has brought me into a conversation with the voices of the Bible, bringing my lived experience and the biblical stories into dialogue in the search for life-giving interpretations. Quaker-shaped Christianity means inhabiting the whole Jesus story as a way to make sense of my life, even the aspects that challenge me. This means I can't avoid those aspects of the Jesus story that I have been wary of, but neither does it mean I have to accept one particular interpretation.

In this book I consider key moments in the Jesus story, exploring how to approach them in life-giving, Spirit-filled ways. But before I can do that, there's one more question I need to ask: Why just the Jesus story? Why only one story when there are so many other stories to choose from?

Chapter 2

Why Only One Story? – Christianity and Universalism

If you ask Quakers to describe their faith and spiritual experience, you'll get a variety of responses. Some Quakers are happy using the word "God," others aren't. Some draw on faith traditions other than Christianity, such as Buddhism or Paganism. Some may prefer not to describe their beliefs at all. Until around the middle of the twentieth century, Quakerism was universally Christian. Today, Quakerism in Britain contains a diversity of belief that can be shocking to people from other Christian churches. This diversity is coupled with a sense that Quakerism is gradually moving in a direction away from Christianity. I often hear Quakerism described as "rooted in Christianity and open to new light," implying that Christianity belongs to the past, and that new, future light comes from non-Christian sources. Quakerism is seen to be in a process of spiritual evolution, outgrowing Christianity and moving towards a universalism that embraces all religious outlooks.

If this is the case, you might wonder why I'm writing specifically about Christianity. Why not write about a universal Quakerism that all Quakers can agree upon? Considering this sense of forward movement, away from Christianity, a book like this might be seen as a step backwards. You may also wonder why I choose to be a Christian in a community with Buddhists and atheists, particularly as being a Christian is rarely something you can do by yourself. In this chapter, I'm going to share why my focus is on one story – the Jesus story – and not many stories, and what it means to be a Christian in a community where not everyone shares my outlook.

The attraction of universalism

Why might universalism be seen as the future of Quakerism? What is its appeal? Universalism is a word with a variety of meanings. Within Christianity, universalism generally means believing that all people will be saved. The first Quakers weren't universalists in this sense, and because Quakers generally shy away from what they see as useless speculation about what happens after death, it's not something Quakers have spent a lot of time discussing. Another meaning of universalism is a belief in the equality of religions, that they all contain aspects of divine truth, and provide access to the same divine reality. This is the type of universalism, also known as pluralism, I'll be discussing in this chapter.

When I began my spiritual exploration in my late teens, I found this type of universalism very attractive. The Christians I'd met saw Christianity as superior to all other faiths, to the point where all non-Christians (even the wrong sorts of Christian) were destined for eternal conscious torment in hell. These beliefs seemed narrow, arrogant and hateful to me. There also seemed to be something odd about God being revealed in a specific person at a particular time in history. If holding the right beliefs was so crucial that wrong beliefs could consign me to hell, it seemed like God was being incredibly unfair in speaking through a single Palestinian two millennia ago. Couldn't God have been spread about more widely? Wouldn't it make more sense for God to be revealed through a variety of cultures?

As well as choosing universalism over what I saw as a narrow Christianity, universalism promised other benefits. History is filled with deadly religious conflict, and embracing universalism seemed to be a step towards peace. Peace is a fundamental Quaker value, and so in a multi-faith world, universalism seems like the most moral option, and a natural belief for a Quaker. A peaceful future can be built on the recognition that there is a common spiritual core shared by all humanity, and that all our various religions are at best decorative, optional extras, and at worst divisive beliefs that keep us apart. A universalism that embraces the Golden Rule of mutual respect and care is surely superior to a world filled with different, conflicting belief systems.

The problems with universalism

There is much to be said for universalism, but I have come to find certain aspects of it problematic. Universalism has been described to me using several metaphors, two of which particularly stick in my mind. The first describes God or Divine Truth as a mountain. Each religious tradition is a different path up the same mountain. The apparent differences between each path are only superficial, because they share the same foundation and goal. They are each journeying to the top of the one mountain. The second metaphor involves an elephant. A team of blindfolded people are attempting to describe the elephant, but each person has taken hold of a different part. One is describing the trunk, another an ear, whilst another is describing a leg. From their descriptions it sounds like they each have hold of wildly different objects, but in fact they are all unknowingly talking about the same creature. These metaphors are saying that, at a fundamental level, every religious tradition is built on the same divine truth. It's also saying that we can only get an accurate picture of divine truth when we take every religious tradition into account. Each religious tradition offers only a limited understanding of a bigger truth.

For the person telling the stories of the mountain and elephant, where are they placing themselves in the scenes they describe? Are they a traveler scaling the mountain, or a blindfolded person groping at a strange, unknown animal? No, in order to describe the mountain with its many paths, the narrator has to imagine themselves standing a long distance away from the mountain, or perhaps flying above the mountain so they can have a "birds-eye view" of all the routes to the summit. Similarly, in order to describe the elephant, the narrator is standing back from the action, without a blindfold. They are privileged with a view of the whole elephant. But if we think about how these metaphors relate to universalism, we then have to ask: is it possible to step back from our situation and see the whole picture? Each one of us occupies a position in time and space. We each embody a particular set of experiences, a specific history. We can't step outside our bodies, our language and culture. The "birds-eye view" or "whole elephant" are never available to us. We can never say with confidence that there is a universal spiritual experience that all faith traditions share. We have no way of knowing. Many in the past have claimed that they can see the big picture, that their understanding of the world is universal. When white European Christians colonized the world, enslaving and displacing indigenous populations, they did so thinking they had a birds-eye view of the world. Believing they were able to stand back from the world and take an objective view, they made their values, customs and skin tone the yardstick with which they measured and judged every stranger and strange land they encountered. Universalism springs from an admirable desire for peace, for equality between faiths, but it accidentally assumes a position of superiority that has its roots in colonialism. The universalist knows a truth that all the religious traditions of the world are yet to realize. The universalist thinks they approach religion in an objective, impartial manner, but to do that they would have to step outside themselves, which is something they can never do. We always speak from a particular cultural perspective. Although the universalism of the mountain and elephant metaphors presents itself as above or separate from the faith communities of the world, as transcending tradition and theology, universalism is itself a tradition and has a theology of its own.

Another problem with universalism is that, by emphasizing

the similarities between all faith traditions, the differences between them are treated as superficial "added extras." In the previous chapter, I wrote how the Judaism of Jesus and the Christianity of the early Quakers aren't "added extras" to an underlying universal message, and I'm going to develop this thought a little further. Focusing on universals means ignoring particulars, the specifics of a religious tradition. This could include religious symbols, festivals, clothing, or ways of praying. When we ignore specifics we get a limited, skewed and inaccurate understanding of different faiths. The things that faith traditions share may not be the most important thing about the tradition for the people within it. Things that are specific to a faith tradition are often highly significant. Take the cross, for example, a specific symbol within Christianity. The cross is absolutely central to the Jesus story, but fades away when we emphasize the commonalities between faiths. In the mountain metaphor, each path heads towards the same destination, but in reality, each faith tradition has its own understanding of the goal of human life. Each has its own definition of "salvation." There are many other differences. Buddhism and Christianity have very different understandings of time and history. The stories told about the God of Mohammed (peace be upon him) in Islam, are very different to those told about the God revealed in Jesus in Christianity, and Buddhism doesn't require God at all. If we truly desire peace between all people, then this can't be achieved by ignoring our differences. In order to treat each faith tradition with respect, we need to take them on their own terms. We need to be able to make peace with each other amidst our differences, accepting that our own understanding of the world is as limited as everyone else's.

Jesus, my place to stand and guiding star

I'm not a universalist, in that I don't believe all religions are different glosses on the same fundamental truth. This still leaves the question of how I relate to other religious traditions, and a Quaker community that contains a wide variety of beliefs. When I first became a Quaker, universalism seemed the most "common sense" option, and was highly preferable to what I understood the Christian position to be. The first Christians I knew who talked openly about their beliefs, told me in no uncertain terms that if I didn't accept Jesus as my personal savior, I would spend eternity suffering in hell. Entrance to heaven required a clean slate, and just a single smudge of wrong doing was enough to deny me entry. By believing a specific abstract truth, that "Jesus died for me," God would forgive me and I was guaranteed eternal life. By implication, people of other faiths and the wrong sorts of Christians were going to burn. Presented with this particularly unpleasant version of the Jesus story, universalism was the more moral option.

I've since discovered that this picture of a sadistic God who demands we sign up to a set of specific, abstract beliefs in order to enter heaven, or escape hell, is only one way of telling the Jesus story. It's a telling that is damaging, and deeply unbiblical. There is no hell to escape, at least not a pit of fire where we'll be skewered by devils for eternity. This sort of hell does not appear in the Hebrew Bible. There is a "land of the dead" called Sheol, but it is simply a place where the dead go. There are ways to interpret references to lakes of fire (e.g., Revelation 20:10), and wailing and gnashing of teeth (e.g., Matt. 13:42) other than as a medieval torture dungeon. The idea of eternal conscious torment is incompatible with the idea of God being Love, or God as just. It makes no sense. If we take this sort of hell out of the equation, this immediately lowers the stakes. I don't need to convert people to my faith to save them from a grisly fate after death.

As well as jettisoning hell, there's also the idea that right relationship with God depends on intellectually assenting to certain beliefs. This needs to be thrown out too. The Christians

I knew at school wanted to me to understand that "Jesus died for me," but the Jesus story gives no indication that God is concerned with precise intellectual formulations like this. Within Christianity, people have held all sorts of varying beliefs about Jesus, and have spent a lot of time arguing about these differences. Who gets to decide which beliefs are the most correct? The emptiness of this focus on "right belief" is most chillingly revealed when we consider that holding "correct," "authorized" beliefs hasn't stopped Christians from committing atrocities, such as white European Christians enslaving black Africans.

So "correct" belief in this sense shouldn't stop me from forming friendships with people of other faiths. There's a temptation at this point to say that, ultimately, our beliefs are irrelevant, and that it's our actions, our behavior that really matters. But this marginalizing of belief altogether steers us back towards the sort of universalism I've been criticizing, which says that the unique beliefs, stories and symbols of a religious tradition are unimportant. To avoid this pitfall, we need to rethink what we mean by "belief." We can't get rid of beliefs. They're inescapable. The idea that actions are more important than beliefs is itself a belief! Because of this, I don't think we can neatly separate beliefs from actions. The stories we tell about ourselves and the world shape how we behave in it. Right action demonstrates right belief, and right belief produces right action. This was a strongly-held conviction of the first Quakers, who believed that we demonstrate our relationship with God through living Spirit-empowered lives. In the Bible we read that faith without works is dead (James 2:17), and that a tree is known by its fruits (Luke 6:44). Jesus said: "Not everyone who says to me, 'Lord, Lord,' will enter the kingdom of heaven, but only the one who does the will of my Father in heaven" (Matt. 7:21). When the Psalmist writes that "fools say in their hearts, 'There is no God,'" the evidence of their foolish unbelief is their "abominable deeds" (Psalms 14:1), not the words they use to describe their religious understanding. Right belief is intimately connected to right action.

If we say "beliefs don't matter," this can lead us into further difficulties. It might lead us to say that all beliefs are equal, of that it's impossible or divisive to discriminate between beliefs. Unfortunately, we can plainly see this is not the case. The world is full of false and harmful beliefs that lead to suffering, violence and injustice. If I'm to live in such a world, I need a way of telling the difference between truth and lies. The marginalizing of belief might also lead us to say that religious beliefs are a private matter. We might think keeping our beliefs to ourselves is a good way to maintain peace in a multi-faith world. For the Jesus story, this can never work. Christianity isn't a private religion, confined to the individual. Jesus lived a public life that attracted all sorts of attention, and died a public, political death. When I say things about God, I'm not making claims about a personal God that only belongs to me. I'm making a public, universal claim. I believe "God is Love" is a fundamental, universal truth. Just as I need a way to tell truth from lies, I need this truth to be publicly championed.

This might sound like I'm contradicting myself. Earlier I criticized universalists for making universal claims, and now I'm saying "God is Love" is universally true. The difference is I'm not claiming to speak from outside a tradition. Rather than attempting to step back from the mountain or the elephant, which is impossible, I accept that I am rooted in a particular faith. In my tradition Jesus is the guiding star, the foundation stone for understanding what right belief and right action looks like. The Spirit of Christ is available to us as a truthful guide (Jn. 16:13), leading us into salvation, which according to Jesus is abundant life (Jn. 10:9). This life is found in the raising up of "the least of these" (Matt. 25:31–46), the hungry and thirsty, the stranger, the poor, the sick and the imprisoned. The Spirit of

Jesus is one of peace and unity (Eph. 4:3). Despite the violence that Christians display and have displayed throughout history, the Jesus story is fundamentally a story of peace. Coercive violence has no part in a Quaker-shaped Christianity. This is a truth that Quakers have maintained for centuries. To be a Quaker-shaped Christian is to treat all others with respect and seek the good of all, regardless of their faith tradition. If the Spirit of Jesus is the Spirit of Abundant Life, then it's a Christian responsibility to support that which is life-giving in all religious paths.

Choosing Jesus as my guiding star doesn't mean I'm closed off to those who don't see Jesus in the same way. There is a type of closure, in that Jesus reveals who God is. In the character of Jesus we glimpse the character of God. God is Love, and that doesn't change. But there is also immense openness. Although Jesus is my center, the horizon of my Christianity is limitless. God is deeper than I can fathom, and broader than I can span. There is always more to learn, and I'm always open to being surprised. A characteristic of the God revealed in Jesus is spaciousness. God is the liberating space within which "we live and move and have our being" (Acts 17:28). The Hebrew Bible repeatedly speaks of God bringing people into a "broad place" (for example, in Ps. 118), symbolizing freedom. The God of Jesus is a God of broad places where people can breathe, live and thrive. I see the holding of different beliefs within the Quaker community as part of this spaciousness. The "broad place" of Quakerism gave me the freedom to explore my spirituality, and eventually become a Christian. This freedom within Quakerism reflects a Divine spaciousness broad enough to encompass all manner of people who have set their hearts on a peaceful and just world, whether they believe in the same God as me or not.

So, do I believe Christianity is the one true faith? The early Quakers certainly thought so. They believed everyone could be saved through responding to God inwardly, to the "inward light," regardless of their religious tradition, but the identity of this inward light was found in Jesus Christ. All those outside Christianity who responded to this light were part of the "Church invisible," as if they were Christians without knowing it. Early Quaker Robert Barclay (1648–1690) wrote in 1678 that the church can include those who are "outwardly strangers and remote from those who profess Christ and Christianity in words" but are "obedient to the holy light and testimony of God in their hearts." At the beginning of the twentieth century, Quakers shifted from believing that Christianity was "the *one* true faith" to "the *most* true faith." It is perhaps only since the 1960s that Quakers have started to see all religions as equally true. I don't think I fit well into any of these positions. The idea that people could be Christians without knowing it feels patronizing, as does the way universalism minimizes the differences between religious traditions. Perhaps the simplest answer I can give is to say that, in my experience, the Jesus story works. Even if there *is* a mountain that we all share, I can only ever see it from the perspective of one path, and the path I've chosen is the one that helps me make sense of the world. The Jesus story excites and inspires me. Jesus challenges me, shows me who God is, and I want to spend my life being his disciple. I long for Quakers to become a community of storytellers – I want to share the Jesus story with my fellow Quakers, and hear the stories that inspire them to work for a peaceful, just world.

There's a danger that, in writing about what the Jesus story means to me in such personal terms, I'm presenting Christianity as an individual philosophy that can be practiced in isolation. Christianity is generally something people do together. Jesus gathered a community around him, and the early Church experienced the Spirit of the Resurrected Christ bringing different people together into a spiritual whole, a new type of family. A central practice of many Christian churches is sharing in bread and wine, eating from the same loaf and drinking from the same cup, with talk of being "one body." To follow Jesus is to be part of the Church, to join in a "community of saints," saints here meaning one of the faithful, rather than an especially good or holy person. With so much in Christianity being about a community unified around the Jesus story, is it possible for me to be a Christian in a Quaker community where Jesus is optional? I admit that this is an important, difficult question, but it must be asked alongside another equally important question: is it possible to be fully myself and be part of the Church? As a gay person, perhaps the majority of Christian spaces are only able to offer me a conditional welcome. I'm accepted only if I leave my same-sex marriage, my gay desires, and my queer sensibilities at the door. My husband and I have occasionally made attempts to find somewhere to worship together, the most recent of which took us to a local church that had many good things going for it: a charismatic, caring pastor, a friendly congregation and a focus on social justice. Despite all this, the church leadership was not united on the acceptability of same-sex relationships. The jury was out on whether same-sex desire and gay love are places where God's abundant love is revealed. I soon realized that I couldn't worship in such a place. I couldn't praise God in a community where I wasn't fully embraced. Each time I went there, a part of me was chipped away. It demanded an unspoken sacrifice, one I wasn't willing to make. So yes, the Jesus story is one that needs to be told, retold and inhabited in community, but as a gay person, I can only do that in a space where I can be fully myself, and my options are limited. In the introduction to this book, I wrote about taking a "patchwork" approach to my faith, supplementing my Quakerism with other types of worship from other Christian traditions. Stitching together a faith life from diverse cloth is a necessity when there are so few places where Jesus is honored and same-sex love and desire celebrated. Within the spaciousness of Quakerism I've carved out a theological niche for myself, one that is rough around the edges, in part because the mainstream Church is yet to offer a box that I fit neatly into. My patchwork blanket of faith may have loose ends, but it gives me the warmth and protection I need to live and thrive. With Jesus as both my place to stand and guiding star, and the broad place I've found in Quakerism, I am open to new discoveries, to friendships across faith traditions, to that which fosters abundant life wherever it is found. There's always room for something new, and I don't need to have all the answers. I am open to new light, light that shines into the present from a Christ-shaped future, which is the focus of my next chapter.

Chapter 3

A Christ-shaped Future

The remaining chapters of this book look at key moments in the Jesus story. These are Jesus' return (known as the Second Coming), his rising from the dead (the Resurrection), his death on the cross (the Crucifixion), and the stories of his birth (the Nativity). I suspect you've noticed two things already. Firstly, I'm telling the story backwards. You might expect me to start with the Nativity, probably the most well-known part of the story considering all the Nativity plays that take place in British schools every Christmas. The Gospels of Luke and Matthew both start with Nativity stories. Why don't I follow their example? I'm starting at the end, because although this is not how the Gospels tell the story, they were written from a post-Resurrection perspective. The Gospel writers weren't documentary makers, following Jesus through his life collecting evidence which they later put together. The significance of Jesus, the reason for telling stories about him, rests on his being risen from the dead. Jesus' disciples continually get Jesus wrong whilst he's alive. It's only when he appears to them after the Resurrection that they fully understand who he is. The ending of a story is often what gives meaning to the whole, and this is particularly true of the Jesus story. The second thing you may have noticed is that there's no chapter on Jesus' ministry, his teaching in and around Galilee and Jerusalem. For people who see Jesus as a historical moral teacher, this is the most important part of the story. Why aren't I including it? I will explore this in more depth in the final chapter, but for now I'll say that Jesus' teaching can't be divorced from the kind of death he died, his Resurrection, and the future this resurrection points towards. Jesus is constantly hinting at the cross, the empty tomb, and the future reign of God, and you could even say that his teaching can only be correctly interpreted through these symbols. I'm beginning with the end of the story, because this is the vantage point from which the rest of the story can be properly understood.

Apocalyptic dangers

When I speak of beginning at the end, which end am I talking about? There are many endings we could refer to. There's the end of our individual lives, the end of the human species, or even the heat death of the universe. When I first encountered Christianity, I was told the end of the story was the destruction of the earth and eternal life spent with God in heaven, or eternal suffering in hell. The ending I'm starting with is what has come to be known as the "Second Coming,", hinted at in Jesus' mysterious words that "they will see 'the Son of Man coming in clouds' with great power and glory" (Mk. 13:26). If you find the words "Second Coming" immediately off-putting, I can understand why. It may conjure up images of God arriving to deal out fiery torment on non-believers, and destroying the world in a nuclear apocalypse. This part of the Jesus story has been interpreted in extremely harmful ways and needs serious rehabilitation.

The end of the world and what happens after death has occupied people throughout history, and there have always been Christians who expected Jesus to return in their lifetime. Predictions for the date of the Second Coming include the years 500, 1000 and 2000. Strangely, what seems to dominate the popular imagination when talking about the Second Coming is not the return of Jesus, but a cataclysmic battle between good and evil. The "apocalypse" – another word closely linked to the Second Coming – has come to mean death and destruction. The antichrist has become a staple of the apocalyptic imagination, despite only occurring in four Bible verses. This figure is seen to signal the "end times," and has been a much-used tool in political struggles, with the medieval Holy Roman Emperor Frederick II, any number of Popes, and even Barack Obama being labeled the antichrist. The number 666 (which appears in only one biblical verse and is most probably a coded reference to the Roman Emperor Nero) has taken on an aura of horror. I was once handed a Christian pamphlet that claimed 666 was secretly hidden in every barcode. Films such as *The Omen* and *Rosemary's Baby* show the fascination we have with this fear-filled understanding of the apocalyptic.

Although the Second Coming has always been a part of the Christian story, it's taken on a particularly horrible intensity in modern times. Today's popular understandings of the Second Coming have their roots in late nineteenth-century evangelical Protestantism, in a movement called "dispensationalism." This is a way of interpreting the Bible, seeing history as divided into several ages or "dispensations." It had its beginnings in the teachings of John Nelson Darby (1800–1882) and became widespread amongst American Evangelicals through the Schofield Reference Bible (1909). Dispensationalism includes a belief in the "rapture," again, based on a single Bible verse. This is the belief that, during the end times, the saved will be snatched away, taken into heaven before a time of tribulation for those who still remain on earth. Despite being such a recent development in Christian thought, the influence of dispensationalism can't be understated, producing such bestselling books as *The Late Great Planet Earth* (1970) and the *Left Behind* series (1995–2007), and even shaping US foreign policy in the Middle East through the political activities of the Christian Right.

Dispensationalism paints a picture of an ultra-violent God, a vision of the future where the earth is destroyed in a fireball, and simplistically divides people into saved and damned, all on the flimsiest of biblical foundations. It's a theology of escape, because the saved can abandon the earth to nuclear annihilation and climate collapse. This is the sort of terrible theology that we need to reject. I want to reject these beliefs, not only because of the harm they do, but because I don't want to allow such beliefs to dictate what Christianity is. Dispensationalism and other life-denying forms of Christianity can't have the last word. I reject these destructive beliefs about the future without rejecting Jesus. I want to counter bad theology with better theology. As I said in Chapter 1, I can't ignore difficult parts of the Jesus story as "added extras." I need to take seriously the way in which Jesus' ministry is directed towards the future, otherwise I'd have to edit out some very large chunks of the New Testament. I need to be able to talk about the future in a way that takes the Bible seriously, and is life-giving in the present. This is what the rest of this chapter attempts to do.

Jesus' ministry and the arrival of God's future

In searching for a life-giving understanding of Jesus' future, I'll start with the term "Second Coming." This is how Jesus' future is often understood. In the Bible, the Greek word that's traditionally translated as "Second Coming" is *parousia*. Unfortunately, this isn't a very good translation! It gives the impression that Jesus has gone away, and will be back again at some point in the future. But the word *parousia* doesn't have a sense of "return." A better translation is "arrival." In Latin, *parousia* is translated as *adventus*, where we get the term "Advent." Advent calendars count down to the "arrival" of Jesus at Christmas. So, I'm going to ditch the phrase "Second Coming" for the rest of this book. Instead, I'm going to speak about God's arrival into the world. I say God's arrival, because, according to the Jesus story, Jesus shows us who God is. This arrival is not a one-off event still to come. It's an arrival that's already in motion. It's a dynamic process. In the Jesus story this process begins at Pentecost, when Jesus' disciples are filled with the Holy Spirit (Acts 2). They experienced this Spirit as the presence of Jesus. The *parousia* begins with the arriving of the Spirit of Christ, and it will be complete when "God is all in all" (1 Corinthians 15:28). Everything between these two points is "the end times." We find ourselves in the midst of God's arriving future.

For those of us who experience God's presence in the everyday and in the natural world, especially Quakers who put such an emphasis on God's presence in the here and now, we might say that God has no need to arrive. God's already here! In one sense I agree. I don't want to suggest that God is somehow absent from the world. It's perhaps better to speak of the arrival of God's reign, or God's promised future. The world today is not how it should be. We hope for something better than the evil and injustice that permeates our lives. There are symbols throughout the Bible that speak of this hoped-for future. There is God's holy mountain where wolf and lamb live in peace with one another, and the earth is full of the knowledge of God (Isaiah 11:6–9). There is the New Jerusalem, a city where there is no poverty, where there is nourishment and healing for all, and where God dwells intimately with God's people (Rev. 21–22). It's a future characterized by spiritual and moral renewal (Ezekiel 36:26), where we will all be fully known, and see each other truthfully (1 Cor. 13). It's a future where there will be justice for all (Matt. 25:31–46).

This is what Jesus' ministry announced. Jesus did not teach a general, present-focused morality. Jesus announced the arrival of a new age called the Kingdom of God, another symbol for God's promised future. This new age belongs to the oppressed, to those who are denied justice, to children, to outcasts, to those on the margins. This Kingdom is not found in royal palaces, but in small, dark places, in mustard seeds, in tiny pearls, hidden in the ground. Jesus placed himself amongst those with mental health issues and the disabled, showing that the Kingdom is found amongst those that the rich consider the "least of these." In this Kingdom, the poor and hungry receive the justice they've been denied, and the wealthy are powerful no longer (Lk. 1:46–55). Because the Kingdom of God belongs to a new age, it reveals the strangeness of the present age to us. Or perhaps it makes us strangers in a strange land. For those of us comfortable with the way the world is, the Kingdom of God brings disruption and disorientation. When we look at the world today, we can see clearly that this Kingdom has not yet fully arrived. Because this arrival is already in motion, we can anticipate God's promised future in the present. Every time peace is made, every time justice is done, whenever we experience plenty and healing, we catch a glimpse of the arriving future. This future is neither completely "now" and neither is it completely "not yet." God's arrival is a dynamic happening that we can taste today. When we taste it, our awareness to present injustice is sharpened, our appetite for peace and justice is whetted, and we are energized to act. This is not a "Second Coming" event to be feared, but an exciting arrival to participate in.

Quakers and God's arrival

If you are familiar with Quakers today, you'll know they rarely speculate about the future. What happens after death, or at the end of time, is not a familiar topic of discussion. This is perhaps because it's seen as useless speculation, or because those whose hold particular beliefs about the afterlife feel embarrassed to share them. It may be all part of the silence Quakers use to cover the theological differences. Because of this silence, it can therefore be a shock to discover that the *parousia* was profoundly important to the first Quakers. They were a community who keenly felt the presence of God's arriving future. They found their intense experience of God's presence reflected in the words of John's Gospel. A lot of familiar Quaker language, such as the "light within" and being a Society of "Friends," comes from John, to the extent of it being called the "Quaker Gospel." John strongly emphasizes the arrival of God's future in the present, such as when Jesus says: "But the hour is coming, and is now here, when the true worshipers will worship the Father in spirit and truth" (Jn. 4:23). The first Quakers found themselves on the knife-edge of the *parousia*. In their experience, the hour had come! They were sharing in the Pentecost experience of God's Spirit being poured out on "all flesh" (Acts 2:17).

This experience had big implications for how they worshiped God. They saw other Christians as still waiting for Christ to come again, and worshipping in "meantime" ways. In their experience, Christ had arrived, meaning that all "meantime" practices had to stop. This included worshiping in a specific building with a set service, being led in worship by a human, male priest, seeing God as especially present in holy water or consecrated bread and wine, and worshipping God on a specific day of the week. With their discovery of God's arrival, Quakers no longer needed to go to a special place. They could worship God "in spirit and truth" wherever they were. A biblical symbol for God's promised future is the New Jerusalem. In this symbolic city there is no temple, because nothing separates God from God's people (Rev. 21:22). The first Quakers saw this reflected in their own experience. They didn't need to go to God, God had come to them. Because the Spirit of Christ was within them, and speaking through them, they didn't need the set prayers and hymns of others. As well as their attitude to Church buildings, or "steeple houses" as Quakers called them, their experience of Christ's intimate presence also shaped their attitude to the priesthood. The priesthood expanded to be a priesthood of all believers (1 Peter 2:9) that included women as well as men. Christ's arrival meant the end of all animosity and division in the community of faith (Galatians 3:28). Friends ministered to one another without the need of a separate priesthood. The worship of Friends was presided over by Christ as their high priest (Hebrews 9). No human being could come between the individual Friend and God. Their understanding of sacraments was also affected. In his first letter to the church in Corinth, Paul writes "for as often as you eat this bread and drink the cup, you proclaim the Lord's death until he comes" (1 Cor. 11:26). In the experience of the first Friends, the Lord had come. They no longer needed to continue with bread and wine communion. Early Quaker theologian Elizabeth Bathurst (1655–1685) wrote that when the Holy Spirit fell upon Jesus' followers at Pentecost, they became filled with the "wine of the Kingdom," wine from Jesus the "true vine" (Jn. 15:1). This meant that "outward" bread and wine was of no use "after Christ's second and spiritual coming," being only a "shadow," whereas inward, spiritual communion is the real "substance." In God's promised future, God is fully present in creation, so God is not especially present in bread, wine or water. God can be found anywhere and everywhere. This is what Quakers mean when they say that the whole of life is sacramental.

Their experience of God's presence led them to see every day as a "Lord's Day," and so they stopped marking Sundays as the Sabbath. Although Quakers have not said much more than this about the Sabbath, we can still see this as part of God's arrival. The Sabbath, the seventh day, is when God rests in God's creation, and when God's creation rests in God. It's a time of wholeness and peace. In the Bible, the number seven always symbolizes completeness and perfection. As well as having a Sabbath on every seventh day, in the Bible there's also another type of Sabbath that happens on a grander scale. This is known as the jubilee (Leviticus 25), which occurs after seven lots of seven years, a total of forty-nine years. This fiftieth year is the jubilee year, a kind of "super Sabbath." It's a year of social and environmental justice when farm land is given rest and left fallow, land is returned to its original owners and slaves are set free. It provides a kind of social leveling, and is so radical that there's doubt it was ever fully put into practice. The jubilee is the "year of the Lord's favor" that the prophet Isaiah proclaims

(Isa. 61), which Jesus in turn announces at the beginning of his ministry (Lk. 4:16–21). Although the Sabbath day and the Jubilee year are part of a repeating pattern, God's arriving future can be seen as an eternal Sabbath, as an everlasting jubilee. These celebrations point towards God's promised future of peace and justice, when all things will experience true rest with God. I say all this because I think the silence and stillness of Quaker worship can be seen as a sign of this rest, and a taste of the eternal Sabbath when "the home of God is among mortals" (Rev. 21:3) and God and creation are at rest in one another. This is something hinted at in the writings of early Friends. James Nayler (1618–1660) wrote that the when the word of God dwells in us, we experience the rest of God's eternal sabbath. It's another way in which Quaker practice points towards a future of intimacy with God, where all divisions have been healed.

The early Quaker experience of God's arrival was so intense that they expected the world to be transformed in their lifetimes. With apocalyptic urgency, Nayler wrote in 1655 that "the Lord is gathering his seed out from the heathen where it hath been scattered, and who will not be gathered, shall be scattered, and who will not come into the kingdom of the Lamb must be left amongst the beasts." But these first Friends were sorely disappointed. Future generations of Quakers had to make sense of this disappointment, and adapt the Quaker vision accordingly. Over the centuries, the *parousia* has receded in the Quaker imagination. Modern Quakers have tried to make sense of the *parousia* by reducing its scope. The biblical vision of God's promised future includes not just humanity, but everything that is, was and will be. It's a vision that includes the living and the dead. This is perhaps too much for modern sensibilities, so the Kingdom has been made smaller. Some confined God's arrival to the mystical experience of the individual, or perhaps the group. According to this approach, we are in the Kingdom when we are spiritually united with the Divine. In mystical experience we can step outside time and history, even outside our own individual identity, into the Eternal Kingdom. The Now of the Kingdom is emphasized, and the not-yet of the Kingdom fades into the background. The difficulty with this emphasis is that it can't make sense of present suffering and injustice. What does it mean to say the Kingdom of God is Now in a world filled with violence, disease and oppression? If our vision of the Kingdom doesn't include everything, it can't be a Kingdom of God. God's future is more than spiritual experience, it's about material justice for all. In mystical experience we can claim to have *tasted* God's Kingdom, but whilst there are still people treated as the "least of these," we can't say that God's future has fully arrived. When we see God's arrival as a dynamic process, as the breaking in of God's future into our present, we can account for both the spiritual intimacy we experience with God now, and the pain and injustice we still see in the world around us and within ourselves. The Kingdom is both now and not-yet. Quaker-shaped Christianity today is about dwelling in this tension, anticipating a Christ-shaped future in concrete ways, making way for God's arrival as midwives of the Spirit of Christ.

Beliefs in a mystical transcending of time into an eternal Now have something in common with modern apocalyptic beliefs, such as dispensationalism and the rapture. They are all theologies of escape. God's promised future is not an escape from this world, or a forgetting of history. The age to come is in direct relationship with the present age. Everything that has been will be gathered up and healed. When God says "See, I am making all things new" (Rev. 21:5), God does not replace one creation with another. It's a renewing, a restoration. The event which shows this connection between the present and God's future is the Resurrection of Jesus, to which I now turn.

Chapter 4

Resurrection

At first, I saw the Resurrection as a barrier to following Jesus. I could connect to his teachings, such as the parables and the Sermon on the Mount, and I could accept Jesus as a human being like me, who, unlike me, was an exceptional moral teacher. I tried to treat the other parts of the Jesus story like optional extras, not central to Jesus' ethical message. The story of Jesus' birth I could (and still do) treat as theological myth – not literally true, but filled with symbolic truth about who Jesus is. The Resurrection didn't feel like that. It resisted my attempts to marginalize it. The Gospel writers are very insistent that the Resurrection actually happened, and Paul writes that the whole of Christianity depends on Jesus actually rising from the dead, going as far as to say that "if Christ has not been raised, your faith is futile" (1 Cor. 15:16). I found this conviction unnerving. I couldn't see why the Resurrection was so necessary to Christianity, feeling it was a superstitious belief we should have grown out of by now. We can plainly see from our own experience that people don't come back from the dead.

My understanding of the Resurrection changed once I began to approach the Jesus story in the way I'm doing in this book – beginning at the end and working backwards. The end of the Jesus story makes sense of everything that goes before. When I approached Jesus chronologically, treating the New Testament writings like a modern biography, I could begin with his birth, or better yet his baptism by John the Baptist and the start of his ministry. This way I could treat his life as that of any other human. I could stop reading before the Resurrection, when things get too weird. But if I start from the vantage point of God's promised future, the Resurrection is cast in a whole new light. This is the perspective of the New Testament writings. They were written after, and in response to, the Resurrection. As I said in the previous chapter, the disciples spend much of their time with Jesus failing to understand what he says. It's only after the risen Jesus appears to them that they fully understand the significance of all he taught them. The Resurrection is what makes Jesus comprehensible. I'm now convinced that if you take the Resurrection out of the Jesus story, it begins to make less and less sense. You're left with a collection of fragments about a failed revolutionary. Take away the Resurrection and it stops being the Jesus story. It becomes a different story entirely.

Making sense of the Resurrection

If Jesus is "risen from the dead," what does it mean to die? Considering how common death is, I'm surprisingly unfamiliar with it. I'm nearly forty years old and, for one reason or another, I've never attended a funeral. I've never seen a dead body. I grew up in a family that didn't talk about death, and in my Quaker community death is mainly spoken about in terms of dying a "good death," or in relation to "assisted dying." When friends speak about death, they say the dead person has gone to a better place, or that they're at peace. This culture of silence, or positivity about death, is at odds with the role death plays in the Jesus story. The God of Jesus is fundamentally associated with life, being both the "living God" (Matt. 16:16) and the God of the living (Matt. 22:32). This God is the creator of all things, of abundant life. In opposition to God, death is as a kind of un-creation. When humanity turns away from God, the source of all life, death enters the world. In death, humanity unravels, returning to the dust from which it was formed (Genesis 3:19). To die is to go to Sheol, a dark, shadowy underworld, a non-place. To be in Sheol is to be separated from God: "For Sheol cannot thank you, death cannot praise you; those who go down to the Pit cannot hope for your faithfulness" (Isa. 38:18). To be without God is a hopeless nothingness. Death also separates us from each other. Loving relationships are broken apart, and broken relationships can no longer be healed. Death prevents future words of love, apology or forgiveness from being spoken. We can speak of natural deaths, or accidental deaths, and all these deaths are painful and profoundly sad in their own ways. In addition to these deaths, throughout history the pain of death has been weaponized as murder, assassination, execution, and war. Those who wield death-dealing powers instill terror, and make those who oppose them disappear. Death prevents true peace from flourishing, and it denies justice to those who die unjust deaths. Because death is an ending, a closing off, a disconnection, there is no hope in death. The despair of death is that, in the end, we will all die, cut off from one another. With no justice or peace, everything will end in nothingness, and that can't be changed. Within the Jesus story, death is the enemy. Death is not something that can be ultimately viewed as a good thing.

The good news of the Jesus story is that life is stronger than death, God is greater than the power of Sheol. God can descend to the grave to be with us (Ps. 139:8), and rescue us (Ps. 86:13). At Jesus' death, the curtain in the Temple at Jerusalem is torn in two (Matt. 27:51). This thick curtain marked the entrance to the Holy of Holies, the innermost sanctuary of the Temple and special dwelling place of God. In being ripped apart, it shows the arrival of a future where there are no barriers between God and humanity (Rev. 21:22) and that "neither death, nor life, nor angels, nor rulers, nor things present, nor things to come, nor powers, nor height, nor depth, nor anything else in all creation, will be able to separate us from the love of God in Christ Jesus our Lord" (Romans 8:38–39). The Resurrection is a promise that is on the side of life. If the power of death separates us from one another, the power of the Resurrection is the healing of relationships. We can see this in Peter's encounter with the risen

Jesus as told by the Gospel of John. Peter is one of Jesus' closest friends, his co-conspirator, and at the Last Supper says he wants to follow Jesus to the end, even at the cost of his life. But after Jesus is arrested, Peter's words are proved hollow when, fearing for his life, he abandons Jesus. Early in the morning, in the light of a charcoal fire, he denies he knows Jesus three times (Jn. 18). These are Peter's last words before Jesus' death. In death, Peter's relationship with Jesus remains broken. The Resurrection of Jesus promises that this is not the end. There is still the opportunity for healing words to be spoken. Early in the morning, by the light of a charcoal fire, Peter meets the Risen Jesus, and confesses his love for Jesus three times (Jn. 21). The Resurrection also shows that death-dealing powers do not have the last word. The powers of Caesar thought that, in murdering Jesus, they were putting an end to him, and instilling the fear of death in his followers. The Resurrection proves that life wins, and the Lordship of Caesar is nothing compared to the Lordship of Christ. Caesar can no longer instill fear, for in Christ there is no fear of death: "'Death has been swallowed up in victory.' 'Where, O death, is your victory? Where, O death, is your sting?'" (1 Cor. 15:54–55).

Importantly, the Resurrection is not just about liberating the living from the fear of death, it also liberates the dead. Those who died unjust deaths will receive justice. This brings us to a part of the Jesus story that Quakers (and perhaps Christians in general) rarely talk about – the general resurrection of the dead. What happened to Jesus will, in the end, happen to all. This was an important teaching of Jesus (e.g., Matt. 22:23–33) his followers (e.g., Acts 4:2), and Paul (1 Cor. 15). This may be the point where the Jesus story becomes too much for modern sensibilities. I'm not asking you to imagine people clambering out of their graves. In fact, I don't know what to imagine! The Jesus story presents the Resurrected life as both familiar and strange. It's familiar in that we will be recognizably ourselves.

There is a continuity between the "old life" and the "new life." The disciples recognize the risen Jesus. His body still does bodily things – he eats and he can be touched. This speaks to the importance of our bodies. They are not a container to be disposed of, or a fleshy prison to be escaped. We are our bodies, and our bodies are us. Jesus' body also still bears the marks of his Crucifixion. He carries his wounds into the new life. This also speaks of the continuity between the old and new life. Just as we don't dispose of our bodies, we don't dispose of our history. The Resurrected life is not an erasure of the past, or a forgetting of our previous lives. In the Resurrected life, everything is brought to light, and the wounds of history are healed. At the same time, the Resurrected life is strange. When the disciples first meet the risen Jesus, it takes them a while to realize that it's him. Earlier I wrote that we can see people don't come back from the dead, but the Resurrection of Jesus is not the reanimation of a dead body. The Resurrection of Jesus has no precedent. There are stories in the Bible of Jesus bringing people back to life, such as Jairus' daughter (Mk. 5:35–43) and Mary's brother Lazarus (Jn. 11:17–27), but these people still died at another point in the future. The Resurrection of Jesus is, in a sense, unimaginable. You could even say that the Resurrection is not a historical event at all. When events happen in history, we can look for and find causes. History is something that humanity makes happen through cause and effect, but the Resurrection of Jesus is not something humanity caused, or humanity can achieve. The Resurrection is entirely God's doing. In this way, the Resurrection is like the Virgin Birth, or the very creation of the cosmos. The hope of life is that things can change for the better, that something new can happen. God announces "See, I am making all things new" (Rev. 21.5), and the Resurrection of Jesus is the crux of this renewal. In raising Jesus from the dead, God is doing a new thing. A new thing is always possible, for all things are possible with God (e.g., Mat. 19:26).

So the Resurrected life is both familiar and strange. It is not a complete break from the old, but neither is it completely new. The new life is the old life, renewed, refreshed and restored. This is what the resurrection of the dead ultimately symbolizes – that in the end there will be healing and justice for all. God's judgment is not about assigning the saved to heaven, and the damned to hell. Rather it is about true justice, the making right of all relationships. If all relationships are to be healed, then all things need to be present. The resurrection of the dead is God wiping away tears from every eye (Isa. 25:8, Rev. 21:4). Ultimately, I must admit that the Resurrection is intensely mysterious. I can't pretend to fully understand it, or offer any cast-iron proof that it happened. I can only say that the Jesus story is incomplete without it, and that it symbolizes real hope for God's future of justice and peace. This hope needs a solid foundation, which is why I think the fact of the Resurrection is crucial – whatever happened, it really did happen. I agree with Paul that without the Resurrection, Christianity is founded on a deception. The empty tomb speaks of this tension and mystery. The tomb was really empty, but we aren't shown what occurred in it. Those who knew Jesus before his death, met him after the Resurrection, but no explanation of how the change occurred was available to them, other than, for God nothing is impossible.

The Spirit of Freedom today

What does this all mean for us today? I've already spoken about the Resurrection as the grounding of hope for the future, but what about the significance of the Resurrection in the present? In the previous chapter I wrote about the process of God's arrival, God's promised future breaking into the present, energizing us with active hope. Although we don't fully share in Christ's Resurrection yet, we can anticipate it today. From a Quaker-shaped Christian perspective, the Spirit we experience in meeting for worship is the Spirit of the Resurrected Christ.

Everything that Christ was and is – his compassion, his righteous anger – we experience through this Spirit. The Spirit of the Arriving Christ that energies us today is also the Spirit of Resurrection. A central way in which the Spirit of Resurrection can be experienced today is as the Spirit of freedom: "Where the Spirit of the Lord is, there is freedom" (2 Corinthians 3:17). The Resurrection releases us from fear, specifically the fear of death, and those who wield death-dealing powers. In the Eastern Orthodox Church, the Easter celebrations are accompanied by the sounds of rattling chains, signifying Jesus breaking open the doors of the underworld. Icons of this story show Jesus bursting through the gates of Hades, dragging Eve and Adam – representatives of all humanity – out of the darkness. Violent powers attempted to silence Jesus by killing him, but the Resurrection proved that the powers of death, violence and oppression will always fail. Jesus repeatedly told his followers not to be afraid, and the Resurrection provides the foundation for that teaching. The last word belongs to a God who is on the side of freedom. Whenever we experience this Spirit of freedom – within ourselves, in our relationships, in our neighborhoods and nations – we experience the Spirit of the Resurrection. When we dwell in the Spirit of the Resurrection, we anticipate a future brimming with freedom. When we are inspired to work for the liberation of all things from unjust systems, it is the Spirit of the Resurrected Christ that drives us forward.

We can experience the Spirit of Freedom in an inward sense. I personally experienced it when I found the courage to come out as gay. Accepting my sexuality allowed me to be fully myself, and the huge weight of fear and self-deception was lifted. I experience the Spirit of Freedom in the freedom to be a follower of Jesus, even when most Christians in the world would say that being a gay Christian is impossible. Just as the grave could not contain Jesus, the Spirit of Freedom spills out of any container we might build for it. My experience of God's love, not in spite

of but because of my queerness, has shown me that the Spirit
of Resurrection is wilder and unrulier than the Church finds
acceptable. In the Gospel of John, Jesus speaks of himself as a
vine. The Spirit of the Resurrected Jesus overgrows any trellis we
might build for it – like the mustard seed of Jesus' parable, it will
eventually take over the whole garden! This abundant freedom
to be myself, and to love God through being queer, is how I
experience the Spirit of the Resurrection inwardly today, and
preach it in my daily life. The first Quakers preached the Spirit
of Freedom through the way they worshipped. Because of the
plainness of Quaker worship, Quakers are sometimes described
in terms of what they don't do – no holy water, no bread and
wine. But Quakerism isn't a list of "don'ts." The plain nature
of Quaker worship is not a restriction of what the Spirit can
do. Rather, it's a recognition that the Spirit can't be contained.
Not having water baptism or bread and wine communion isn't
a denial of the power of those symbols. It says that what they
symbolize isn't limited to those symbols. The spiritual renewal
associated with the waters of baptism can happen without
those waters. Communion with God can occur wherever God
chooses and people are open to that communion. I have found
God in the bread and wine of the Eucharist, in pizza shared at
a birthday party, in the curry ladled out at an anti-arms trade
demonstration, in a tray of shots at my favorite gay bar, in tea
and biscuits shared with refugees and asylum seekers, and in
the silence of Quaker worship. God is free to meet us, love us
and gather us together at whatever time God chooses.

As long as the freedom of the Spirit is purely inward and
spiritual, it remains incomplete. It can't be restricted to a
sense of personal freedom. Quaker-shaped Christianity is not
a mystical way of detaching ourselves from our embodied
existence in history. The freedom of the Spirit is both spiritual
and material, individual and social. God is the God of the
living, not of disembodied spirits. Our bodies are not vessels

to be escaped. The resurrection of the dead means that God's future includes our whole being, body and all. We anticipate the resurrection in a material way by loving our bodies. As a fat teenager, I saw my body as an embarrassment, as something highly undesirable. The more I dwell in the Spirit of Freedom, the more I love my body as it is and see myself as lovable. As well as human bodies, all non-human bodies are included in the Spirit of Resurrection. The apostle Paul taught that the freedom of the rest of creation is bound up with our own freedom. The creation groans to be free, and hopes "to obtain the freedom of the glory of the children of God" (Rom. 8:21). Birds, insects, flowers, mountains, oceans and stars are our companions. We are part of a community of creation meant to enjoy freedom together. The freedom of the Spirit means loving life in all its forms. If we love our bodies, our fellow humans, and the rest of the creation, then we will be compelled to work for the freedom of all. We anticipate the Resurrection in a social way by struggling for reconciliation and justice between all things in the here and now. My freedom is bound up with your freedom, our freedom with their freedom. I can't be satisfied with my own freedom as a white, gay man in the UK. I need to ask how other queer people still face discrimination, and how my country treats LGBT+ asylum seekers. Being inspired by the Spirit of Resurrection doesn't reconcile us to the way things are. Its light shows us how much our present reality does not match the Christ-shaped future of the Jesus story. It's a wake-up call to the strains and struggles of history. Those Quakers who have been moved to work for peace and justice know this. We don't have to choose between a life of prayer or a life of action. Our material liberation and our spiritual liberation go hand in hand. The spiritual power of God's freedom equips us to work for the holistic freedom of all today. This is why we can't just sit back and wait for the promise of the Resurrection to be fulfilled. If we are not living a life that actively anticipates everything the Spirit of Resurrection promises – inwardly and outwardly – then we haven't fully grasped what it means to be alive in Christ. In a world full of greed and oppression, freedom doesn't come to us for free. In the Jesus story, the costliness of freedom is found in the cross, the subject of the next chapter.

Chapter 5

Crucifixion

The other side of the Resurrection is the Crucifixion. If the Resurrection is freedom from death-dealing powers, and the freedom to love all life, then the Crucifixion means facing all the ways we hate, discard and deal out death to one another. To confront why Jesus died as a victim of state torture and execution is to confront human evil. In this chapter, I begin by describing my own difficulties with how the Crucifixion gets talked about. I go on to explain how I find the concept of sin helpful, and what the cross means to me today.

My problems with the cross

Like the *parousia* and the Resurrection, the cross is another tricky part of the Jesus story, although for very different reasons. I could dismiss the *parousia* and Resurrection of Jesus because they seemed like superstitious, "supernatural" additions to the story, myths that distract from the core message of Jesus' teachings. In contrast, the idea that Jesus was crucified is perfectly believable. If we can be sure of any historical detail of Jesus' existence, it's that he was crucified by the Romans. This is something Christians and non-Christians agree on. You could say it's the hard reality of the cross that makes it so difficult. That this horrible, violent event occupies a central place in Christianity is hard to deal with. Entering churches as a child, I was always confronted with a picture or sculpture of a dead man's corpse on an instrument of torture. If the important thing about Jesus was his moral teaching, why were Christians so fixated on this shocking, morbid image?

Growing up, I picked up answers to this question from Christians I knew. The consensus seemed to be that God needed

Jesus to die in this horrible way, and in dying an unimaginably painful death, Jesus died for me. I found this incomprehensible. If God is a God of peace – something I felt instinctively, and heard Christians claim – why would God require such horrific violence? In my brief stint as a Cub Scout, I attended a Remembrance Day church service with a giant red poppy placed in front of the pews. The vicar explained that the black center of the flower represented the blackness of our sin, the red petals were Jesus' blood shed for us, and the green leaf the new life that could be found in Jesus. I remember this event vividly, and I'm still shocked at the crassness of this message. As a child in the pews, I was confused. I thought the point of remembering dead soldiers was to remember "never again," but the Church was telling me that the shedding of blood was a good thing. If God required the death of God's Son, did that make God a murderous, abusive parent? Or if Jesus was God, did that mean God was self-harming? On hearing the message that Jesus died for me, my immediate response was "But I don't want him to!" I don't want anyone to suffer that way on my behalf. If Jesus paid the price for my sins, what could I have done that's so bad that Jesus needed to die in such a horrible way? The Crucifixion seemed to put violence at the center of who God is.

If the Crucifixion made violence central to God's identity, it also made shame central to mine. If Jesus died in my place, then it's me who deserves to be crucified. Being a Christian seemed to involve being consumed with shame. A Christian I knew at school related a sermon they'd heard at church. The vicar invited members of the congregation to put their hands through a hole in a shoe box, not knowing what they would end up touching. Inside the box was something slimy and slug-like, something that would make you draw your hand back quickly, something you didn't want to touch. The point of the sermon, as I heard it, was that God is gracious to us by reaching out to touch us, in spite of our slimy, disgusting and untouchable nature. The Christian telling me this seemed to think it was good news. All I heard was "loving God means feeling disgusting and untouchable." Another Christian friend told me that you could only get into Heaven with a clean slate, and any sin, no matter how small, counted against you. Ludicrously, this meant that all sinful actions were equally bad in the eyes of God: a jealous thought was equivalent to genocide. As far as I was concerned, the gateway to Christianity meant the taking on of unbearable shame. Why would anyone choose such a path? Thankfully, my loving parents gave me a strong sense of self-worth. When I looked inside myself, I wasn't filled with shame and self-disgust. At 17, my door to faith was an overwhelming sense of the universe being filled with Divine Love. Joy in the wonder of the world opened my eyes to God. I recognized as true that "the heavens are telling the glory of God" (Ps. 19.1). It was at my wedding that I began to understand God's grace. I looked around me and thought "this is so wonderful. How could anyone deserve something this good?" And then it clicked: talk of who deserves what isn't how God works. God makes the sun "rise on the evil and on the good, and sends rain on the righteous and on the unrighteous" (Matt. 5:45). I was opened to grace through abundant love, not guilt. This meant that, for a long time, the cross felt alien to me, and it took many years for me to understand its place in the Jesus story.

Salvaging sin-talk

I'm sure I'm not the only one who has difficulties with the cross. The way the cross, sin and evil have been talked about has a difficult history. People have been damaged by sin-talk, taking deeply into themselves feelings of shame and self-hatred, and a fear of God as a violent and unjust parent. The language of sin has been used as a tool of spiritual abuse. I often meet people who come to Quakers to escape harmful theology like this, who have understandable difficulties with talk of the Crucifixion and evil. For these people, Quakerism is a safe haven from sin-talk. There are perhaps good historical reasons for this. From the very beginning, Quakers rejected the idea that we were born guilty and deserving of God's punishment. The first Quakers believed that salvation for all people was possible before death. In the twentieth century, Quakers began to emphasize the inherent goodness of human beings, and talked less and less about our capacity for evil. Today, sin-talk is unusual amongst Quakers, and that has its benefits. When first exploring my spirituality as a young gay person, I needed a community who accepted every part of me. When I came out to a Christian school friend, she refused to acknowledge what I'd shared with her. She attempted to continue our conversations as if my sexuality had never been mentioned. She wanted to remain friends, but ignore my being queer. From my perspective, this was impossible. It felt like she was trying to "love the sinner, hate the sin," a phrase that's sadly familiar to many queer Christians. She wanted to reject something that was a fundamental (and fundamentally good) part of me. My Quaker community, free of sin-talk and affirming of my goodness, was a welcome relief from this sort of contorted prejudice. For those who recoil from sin-talk, Quakerism has become a safe space. A sin-talk free space can be useful, for a time, but I came to realize that abandoning sin-talk altogether leaves us at a disadvantage. What sin-talk gives us is a language strong enough to capture the seriousness of human evil. How are we to talk about genocide, greed, oppression and tyranny, without the language of sin? It's important to acknowledge the way sin-talk is used as a tool of spiritual abuse, and at the same time, I find "sin" and "evil" to be the strongest words we have to describe the seriousness of such abuse. Sin-talk allows me to name homophobia as sin. Sin-talk is useful because it's so difficult.

I think sin-talk is an indispensable part of our theological toolbox, but because of its harmful history, it needs to be adapted in two ways before we can use it safely. We firstly need to move from talking about individual "sins" and individual "sinners," to talking about sin as a system. I grew up thinking sin was about individual acts. A sin was something you did or didn't do. If you did a sinful thing, you were a sinner. This can lead us to become overly concerned with our own moral purity, constantly asking ourselves "am I sinning or not?", becoming guilt-stricken over the most trivial of things. Of course, there are actions we can point to and name as plainly evil, but these actions don't exist in a vacuum. They emerge from a tangled web of brokenness. We constantly shape and are shaped by a complex network of relationships. Because of this, I think sin is better thought of as a state of being. Sin is the broken, tangled nature of the web. Sin is like a sticky residue that gets everywhere, or like an infectious, debilitating disease. Think of the climate crisis we are experiencing. As much as I might try to recycle or compost, my way of living actively fuels climate chaos. I'm part of a system that disregards the non-human creation, a system I can't fully extract myself from. Focusing on my individual sins or good deeds is not going to make much of a difference. Or think of racism and white supremacy. I was born into a system that privileges people with pale skin. As a white person, I've soaked this system up, and I replicate it in all sorts of small ways that I'm unaware of. I unconsciously make decisions and take actions that are affected by racism.

The danger with seeing sin as a system is that we abandon any sense of personal responsibility. If we do this, we forget that systems are made up of people. The systemic evil of white supremacy shapes individuals, and at the same time is sustained by individuals. I'm shaped by racism, and my actions perpetuate racism. In the Jesus story, sin-talk done right holds the systemic nature of sin in tension with how this system is expressed and perpetuated by individuals. It explains how I can unconsciously do wrong, and still be responsible for the harm my actions do.

When thinking of sin as a system I'm part of, as the ocean I swim in, Paul's words about sin make much more sense to me: "I do not understand my own actions. For I do not do what I want, but I do the very thing I hate" (Rom. 7:15). When Paul does the very thing he hates, it is still him doing that thing. He is responsible, even if he doesn't understand his actions. This helps explain how the evils of this world are mostly perpetuated or enabled by very normal people who are "just doing their job" or who only want a quiet life. A Quaker who saw the systemic nature of sin clearly was John Woolman, who exhorted Friends to examine their way of life and their possessions for the "seeds of war." "Ordinary" ways of living can feed all manner of injustices. Sin describes the violent, oppressive disorder we see in the world, and how that disorder is present in our own lives. It's a way of talking about our own brokenness, and how this brokenness is present inwardly and personally, in our social relationships, and within the wider creation.

The second adaptation that needs to be made if we are to rehabilitate sin-talk, is that we need to have an unshakeable sense of our own self-worth, grounded in God's love. We can't talk about sin in a healthy way without being anchored in a sense of our own goodness. Without this step, sin-talk can descend back into destructive self-hatred and shame. What is the foundation of our goodness? I grew up with an aching desire to be good, to be approved of. I thought that my goodness was related to the good things I did. The more good things I did, the better a person I was. This led me into an unhealthy spiral of continually trying and failing to be perfect. When I eventually let go of this need for perfection and goodness it was a transformative experience. In this experience I discovered my goodness is founded not on my good deeds, but on being part of God's good creation. All good things come from God, and I'm one of those things. Just by our existence we are evidence of God's goodness. When Quakers talk about "that of God in everyone," this includes a sense that we are good because we are God's children. This is what Jesus meant when he said "why do you call me good? No one is good but God alone" (Mk. 10:18; Lk. 18.19). The whole of God's creation is good because it participates in the goodness of its Creator. In accepting myself as good in this way, I can honestly examine the depths of my own racism, without my goodness being threatened. To recognize the ways I'm shaped by white supremacy, to accept that in many ways I am racist, doesn't mean going to a place of self-hatred. My grounding in God's goodness gives me a secure place from which to face the sinful nature of the world and my place in it.

When we affirm our innate goodness and our sinful disorder, we can both love ourselves and recognize all the ways we participate in, and perpetuate evil systems. We can see how a person can do many good things, and at the same time have problematic views, be a bystander to evil, or commit terrible evil themselves. You can think you're actively pursuing good, but be perpetuating racism or homophobia. Jesus was executed by people who believed they were doing the right thing by maintaining law and order. We can't divide the world into saints and sinners. More often than not, we're both at the same time.

What the cross says

Rehabilitating sin-talk in this way, I can now offer a Quaker-shaped Christian perspective on the Crucifixion. In the Jesus story, the cross is God's response to sin. The cross in some way frees us from sin. In trying to make sense of this, I find it helpful to think of the cross having an outward and an inward dimension. The outward dimension is the cross of wood and nails, which the Romans used as a form of state execution. In being crucified, Jesus died a public, political death. The cross shows that the Kingdom of God can't be confined to a private, spiritual realm. The Kingdom of God is not restricted to being a good citizen. The cross isn't an answer to personal, private sin, but to sin on a grand scale. The good news of the Kingdom is a political threat to those who benefit from systemic sin. If we are to follow the Way of Jesus, seeking God's Kingdom before all else, we should be prepared to meet resistance from powerful forces. In the previous chapter, I wrote that the promise of the Resurrection doesn't mean we can sit back and wait for the Kingdom to arrive. The cross, as the other side of the Resurrection, shows the seriousness of the struggle for a Christ-shaped future. It shows the costly nature of discipleship. It's important to say that there's nothing inherently virtuous about suffering. The Crucifixion didn't have to happen, and God doesn't require Jesus' death. There's always a danger of the Crucifixion being used to justify suffering. But in some sense Jesus' Crucifixion was inevitable. The death-dealing powers can't countenance the existence of God's Kingdom, and so will always try to destroy it. The first Quakers knew this outward Crucifixion well. Their announcement of Christ's arrival was met with violence, torture and imprisonment. They were a political threat. Some, like Mary Dyer in Boston, received state executions. Quakers in Britain still have a "Meeting for Sufferings" which has reprised its historical role of recording Quakers who suffer imprisonment for their witness. We still understand that suffering is to be risked if there is to be real change for the better. The cross also demonstrates the hypocritical, fallen nature of the death-dealing powers. It reveals the "way things are" to be a system of sin. The Romans who executed Jesus claimed their rule brought peace, but the cross shows the peace of Rome to be built on the shedding of innocent blood. At the Crucifixion the greatest empire in the world put an innocent man to death for the sake of "law and order" and the "public good." The cross is a judgment on all the systems of sin we inhabit, on all the ways that the good of some rests on the exploitation and oppression of others.

The inward dimension of the cross is what occurs in the heart. The inward dimension asks "What does the cross say about God?" The cross shows us where God is. In Jesus, God suffers and dies on the cross, and so is with those who suffer and die on all the crosses throughout history. The cross demonstrates God's solidarity with the oppressed, with everyone who is marginalized and scapegoated. The cross shows that Christianity is not a faith of positive thinking or self-improvement. God isn't found with the successful and prosperous. God is with those who are at the end of their tether, who have nothing left. God is with those who say with Jesus, "God, why have you abandoned me?" For the crucified, this inward dimension of the cross is experienced as a comfort. For those in an alliance with the crucifying powers, the experience is very different. The cross shows that God is against those who crucify. The cross is experienced as a personal judgment. This is how Quakers have traditionally known the cross. The inward experience of the cross is dying to a reliance on the death-dealing powers of the world. The demons of racism and homophobia have to be exorcised. The poison of transphobia and ableism has to be expelled. The "seeds of war" have to be uprooted. This inner work hurts. This is why the first Friends "quaked" – they experienced the cross as a spiritual earthquake that exposed their participation in the crucifying systems of sin. The Light showed them their darkness, and it dramatically "shook the hell out" of them.

The inward and the outward dimensions need to be held in tension. We don't need to make a choice between being a mystic or being an activist. The way of Jesus involves both. Just as the Resurrection proclaims spiritual and material freedom, the Crucifixion proclaims that the struggle for God's Kingdom is political and personal, outward and inward. The Quaker activist knows they cannot rely on their own power, especially in the shadow of the outward cross. Through prayer and worship they draw on a strength that is beyond themselves. If we are to love God with all our heart, soul, and strength (Deuteronomy 6:5), then using all our gifts and skills and emotions in pursuit of a better world is itself an act of worship. To be an activist is to be a mystic. The Quaker mystic allows the light to shine on their darkness. They open themselves to the pain of the world, to the inward cross, and suffer with it. This compassion is what moves them to work for change. Contemplation is itself an action. It's something you do, and it can be hard work. You could even say that prayer and worship are political acts. To open ourselves to God is to acknowledge an authority higher than the political powers of this world. For the Early Christians, saying "Jesus is Lord" meant that Caesar was not the god he claimed to be. To be a mystic is to be an activist.

It is worth returning to the Resurrection at this point, for we say that God is on the cross, on the lynching tree or in the gas chamber, but go no further, we might ask "so what?" If all God can do is suffer with the oppressed whilst the powerful do what they want, exploiting the poor and poisoning the earth, then what use is God? This is why we can't talk of the Crucifixion without the Resurrection. They are two sides of the same coin. In the Crucifixion we see the powerful do their worst to Jesus; in the Resurrection we see that their worst wasn't enough. The cross is the powerful saying "No" to the Kingdom of God; the Resurrection is God saying "Yes." The cross is the reminder that the struggle for the Kingdom of God might cost us everything; the Resurrection is the assurance that, we may lose everything in the struggle, but we can never be separated from God.

I wrote this chapter with a sense of my own unworthiness. What can I, a privileged white man who lives a comfortable life, possibly say about the cross? I've attended anti-arms trade demonstrations and peace vigils, but in all honesty, what can I say I've risked for God's Kingdom? I see the cross as a central, deeply uncomfortable challenge. An image of the Crucifixion I'm particularly challenged by is the picture of Jesus on the cross, with the criminals crucified on his right and left. At the foot of the cross are the women followers of Jesus, sometimes named as the Three Marys. Other Christian thinkers have prompted me to see this as an image of the Church – a community of the crucified, and those in solidarity with the crucified. This image prompts me to ask continually: Who are the people being crucified now? How am I in solidarity with them? Where do I need to go to be at the foot of the cross?

Chapter 6

Planting a Seed

Having begun at the end of the Jesus story with the *parousia*, and traveled backwards through the Resurrection and Crucifixion, this final chapter deals with beginnings. This is a chapter about seeds. There's a tradition of speaking of Jesus in horticultural terms. One of my favorite Christmas carols speaks of "Jesus Christ the apple tree," and Jesus describes himself as the "true vine." If we can speak of Jesus as a vine and a tree, we can also speak of him as a seed. As I draw the threads of this book together, I reflect on the seed in three related ways. First, I reflect on what could be thought of as a seed of the Jesus story, the Nativity. Second, I explain how "Christ the seed" was an important idea for the first Quakers, an idea that is ripe for Quakers to reclaim today. Third, I look to Mary, mother of Jesus and bearer of Christ the seed, and a key character in the Nativity story.

Nativity

The beginnings of Jesus' life are told in the Gospels of Matthew and Luke. In moving from the Crucifixion to the Nativity, I've missed out a potential chapter on Jesus' ministry, his time teaching and healing in Galilee and Jerusalem with his disciples. My earlier self would be very critical of this, and would say I've missed out the most important part of the story. As I've already said, I now see the whole of Jesus' ministry as pointing towards, and contained within, his Crucifixion, Resurrection and God's arriving future. The Gospels were written in the light of the Resurrection. Everything they have to say is a commentary on Jesus as the Risen Christ. Jesus' healings, exorcisms and teaching all point to the arrival of God's Kingdom. I also see this in the stories of Jesus' birth. Although the Nativity stories may contain some historical elements, I read them as a projection of Jesus' mission, ministry and character back into an "origins" story. The cross, the Resurrection and *parousia* cast their light back into the past, so that the Nativity stories "foreshadow" everything that Jesus will be. The Nativity is a seed of the whole Jesus story, a microcosm of what is to come.

We see the shadow of the cross in Simeon's words to Mary that Jesus "is destined for the falling and the rising of many in Israel, and to be a sign that will be opposed so that the inner thoughts of many will be revealed—and a sword will pierce your own soul too" (Lk. 2:34–45). In these words we hear how the death-dealing powers will violently resist God's Kingdom, and how the cross reveals the systems of sin that live inside us. Mary, who will one day be with her son at the foot of the cross, is told of the costly, painful nature of solidarity with the crucified. We also see the shadow of the cross in Herod's response to the news of God's coming reign. In Matthew's Gospel, Jesus is portrayed as a second Moses, and so Herod becomes a second Pharaoh. Just as Pharaoh attempts to murder the Hebrew children (Ex. 1), Herod slaughters the children of Bethlehem (Matt. 2:16). The Kingdom of God is a threat to those who thrive on systems of sin, and it will be violently opposed by the death-dealing powers.

We see the light of the Resurrection in the miraculous, strange nature of Jesus' birth. Both the Virgin Birth and the Resurrection rest on the fact that nothing is impossible with God (Lk. 1:37). In his birth, as in his Resurrection, God is doing a new thing (Isa. 43:19) as God will make all things new (Rev. 21:5). In the Resurrection we see the removal of all barriers between God and humanity. In the Nativity we see this both in Jesus' title "Emmanuel," meaning "God is with us," and in the veil between heaven and earth being lifted as the angels appear to the shepherds.

We see God's promised future arriving in Jesus as the Messiah, the Christ who ushers in God's Kingdom. The Nativity stories make much of Jesus as the royal, Messianic "Son of David": "He will be great, and will be called the Son of the Most High, and the Lord God will give to him the throne of his ancestor David. He will reign over the house of Jacob forever, and of his kingdom there will be no end" (Lk. 2:32–33). This is why Jesus is born in Bethlehem, the city of David (Lk. 2:4). As well as the naming of Jesus as the Messiah, the character of God's Messianic Kingdom is made clear. In the Kingdom of God, the proud and powerful are humbled, and the powerless are lifted up. The hungry are fed, and the rich realize their wealth cannot help them (Lk. 1:51–53). The Kingdom of God is a light in the darkness, and "the way of peace" (Lk. 1:79). In the Kingdom, God's promise to the people of Abraham and Jacob is expanded, embracing those beyond the borders of Israel (Lk. 2:32). The surprising, strange nature of the Kingdom is shown in the foreign "wise men" expecting to find Jesus in a palace. In bringing their treasures to honor Jesus they echo the foreign nations bringing their "glory and honor" into the New Jerusalem (Rev. 21:26). The Kingdom of God is a place of peace and reconciliation.

The seed of Christ within

There is a strong Quaker tradition of using the metaphor of a seed to describe the religious life. The first Quakers spoke of "Christ the seed," drawing on a familiar Christian symbol with biblical roots. As a Quaker-shaped Christian, I find the seed to be a very helpful theological tool. Quakers today are more familiar with the symbolism of the "inner light," but our Quaker language could be further enriched by a reclaiming of the "seed within."

In the Bible, particularly in the King James translation familiar to the first Quakers, the seed is an agricultural metaphor for the Kingdom of God. The Kingdom is like a mustard seed, apparently insignificant in its smallness but with potential to become "the greatest among herbs" (Matt. 13:31–32). In Jesus' story of the sower, the seed of the Kingdom is sown scattered on all types of ground, just as it's sown into all hearts. Some hearts receive the Kingdom and others don't (Matt. 13:1–9, 18–23). The seed is also used to speak about human offspring and descendants, such as when God established a covenant with Noah "and with your seed after you" (Gen. 9:9). In the New Testament, this image is used to symbolize the way in which the followers of Jesus experience a new birth, becoming children of God: "Being born again, not of corruptible seed, but of incorruptible, by the Word of God which liveth and abideth for ever" (1 Pt. 1:23). To be born of God is to have God's seed within you (1 John 3:9). The first Quakers also drew on Genesis 3:15, where God says to the serpent which tempted Eve, "I will put enmity between thee and the woman, and between thy seed and her seed; it shall bruise thy head, and thou shalt bruise his heel." Quakers followed other Christians in connecting this passage about the woman, her seed and the serpent with a passage from the last book of the New Testament, Revelation. This speaks of "a woman clothed with the sun," the child she bears and "a great red dragon" (Rev. 12:1–3). This red dragon is the enemy of the woman, "and went to make war with the remnant of her seed, which keep the commandments of God, and have the testimony of Jesus Christ" (Rev. 12:17). The passage from Genesis, which is about the breakdown in relationship between humanity and the non-human creation, is reinterpreted as being about the cosmic struggle between the followers of Jesus Christ (the "seed" of the Mary, the new Eve) and the forces of evil (the red dragon).

The first Quakers wove this biblical material into a way of speaking about their religious experience. Like the Nativity story, they saw the seed as filled with potential, as bigger on the inside. The seed was able to contain a host of other biblical images within it, such as God's Word, Kingdom, Spirit and

Gospel. "Seed" and "light" are used interchangeably, and the seed is spoken of as revealing our inward condition in the way the light does. Isaac Penington (1616–1679) wrote "God is light; and this seed, which comes from him, is not darkness, but light; and in the springing light of this seed, God and Christ are revealed." In Penington's words, the seed springs from "the womb of the heavenly wisdom" and God, in and through Christ, sows the seed in the dark, secret "inward earth" of every human heart, just as the light of Christ enlightens everyone.

As well as the seed of God, early Friends also spoke of the "seed of the serpent." This represented the human potential for sin and moral weakness, the power of death and everything that separates us from God. To accept the seed of God means to struggle against the seed of the serpent. Margaret Fell (1614–1702), in her tract "Women's Speaking Justified," writes that those who oppose women preaching are siding with the seed of the serpent: "Let this Word of the Lord, which was from the beginning, stop the Mouths of all that oppose Women's Speaking in the Power of the Lord; for he hath put Enmity between the Woman and the Serpent; and if the Seed of the Woman speak not, the Seed of the Serpent speaks."

As in the parable of the sower, the inward earth of our hearts is often not suitable for the seed of God to grow. It may be rocky or choked with thorns. When we rely on our own resources, and not on God, then, in the words of James Nayler, "the seed of God is in prison." Penington writes that, for the seed to grow, we must allow God to plough up the stony ground of our hard hearts, rooting up evil. George Fox (1624–1691) had a vision of a great, smoking earthquake, which he interpreted as "the earth in people's hearts which was to be shaken before the Seed of God was raised out of the earth." Then, through this "quaking" of the heart, opening it to God, the seed can be stirred to life by the Spirit. Nayler writes that in silent worship, waiting in the light, we become aware of the seed which is "breathing" in us after God, like a deer panting for water (Ps. 42:1). Then "that seed is raised, the bonds of death are broken, the way of life is found."

Once accepted, the seed contains everything needed for a devout, holy life, although it is initially hidden because of the smallness of the seed. From Christ the seed come the fruits of the Spirit (Gal. 5:22–23) and the blessings promised by Jesus (Matt. 5:1–12). The seed unites us with God, and with everyone else who is united to the seed "for the promise is to the seed which is one, not to seeds which is many" (Gal. 3:16). The seed contains the experience of the inward cross, for the seed destroys everything that separates us from God, including any illusion we may have of being independent from God. The seed also leads us to the outward cross, for the life of the seed will bring us into conflict with the powers of death. Nayler, who himself suffered terribly for his witness, wrote that because the seed of the Kingdom is very small, it is "trodden underfoot by the kingdoms of the world" and makes those who bind themselves to it strangers and pilgrims in the world.

Importantly, the seed has the potential to grow. Sometimes we can talk about the light in a way that feels static. There's a dynamism, a direction to the seed, that feels exciting. Elizabeth Bathurst makes it clear that both the seed and the light are symbols of growth when she writes that "the Seed (or Grace) of God, is small in its first appearance (even as the Morning Light) but as it is given heed to, and obeyed, it will increase in Brightness, till it shine in the Soul; like the Sun in the Firmament at its Noon-day height." In keeping with this sense of growth, early Friends described the seed as a "measure," and connected it to the parable of the talents (Matt. 25:14–30). The intention for the seed is that it will germinate. The intention for us is that we will be renewed, changed and transformed. To feel the seed grow in us, to grow with the seed, is to grow up in Christ. The seed grows in us like rising bread, it cleanses us like fire and water, it purifies us like salt. We become like a field in which is hidden a pearl of great price (Matt. 13:44–46). Robert Barclay wrote that "as the whole body of a great tree is wrapped up potentially in the seed of the tree, and so is brought forth in due season; and as the capacity of a man or a woman is not only in a child but even in the very *embryo*, even so the Kingdom of Jesus Christ, yea Jesus Christ himself, 'Christ within, who is the hope of glory,' and becometh wisdom, righteousness, sanctification and redemption, is in every man's and woman's heart, in that little incorruptible Seed, ready to be brought forth as it is cherished and received in the love of it." In words much loved by Quakers today, Penington urges us to "sink down to the seed which God sows in the heart, and let that grow in thee, and be in thee, and breathe in thee, and act in thee, and thou shalt find by sweet experience that the Lord knows that, and loves and owns that, and will lead it to the inheritance of life, which is [God's] portion."

What would Mary do?

There is one difficulty I have with the early Quaker image of the seed. From the way these Quakers speak about the seed, it sounds as if the seed contains the whole universe within it. To possess the seed is to want for nothing else. But seeds don't contain everything they need to grow. They need sunlight, water, and nutrients from the earth. Similarly, we don't contain everything we need within us as individuals to grow spiritually. None of us are spiritually self-sufficient. This has implications for how we read the Jesus story. Because we can't talk about the seed in isolation from the earth and the rain, we can't talk about Jesus by himself. We can't talk about Jesus without Judaism, and we certainly can't talk about him without Mary his mother. To close a book about Quakerism by talking about Mary might feel odd. It might feel more Catholic than Quaker. For those who dismiss the Nativity stories because of their mythical nature, it can be easy to ignore Mary too. Too strong a focus on Jesus, at the expense of others in the Jesus story, can lead to problems. It's very common for Christians to identify with Jesus. The early Quaker experience of the Inward Christ was such that they were accused of claiming to *be* Jesus. "What would Jesus do?" still feels like a natural question to ask when discerning how to act, especially for people who see Jesus chiefly as a moral teacher. However, history is filled with white men like me who've identified themselves with Jesus, and by implication with God. I think it's time to try a different question: "what would Mary do?"

In Mary's story, we can see the upside-down nature of the Kingdom of God. She is a teenage, brown, Jewish girl, and comes from a Palestinian backwater with a bad reputation (Jn. 1:46). She will soon become a refugee, giving birth not in a palace, but amongst animals. She is all this, and she is chosen to reveal God. A title for Mary in the Eastern Orthodox church is "God-bearer." In carrying Jesus in her womb, she contained God within her. In the Bible, the presence of God is such that humanity cannot witness it and live (Ex. 33:20), but Mary contained God and wasn't consumed. She is like the Unburnt Bush (Ex. 3), aflame with God without being destroyed. Mystics have seen Mary as a model of Christian spirituality. Like Mary we can bear Christ within us and birth God into the world. The early Quakers didn't talk about Mary in this way, possibly because of the strong anti-Catholic prejudices of the time, but they did talk about Christ the Seed, and the Inward Christ. To me, there are natural parallels between the Quaker spirituality of Christ the Inward Seed, and Mary the God-bearer. There are also resonances with the Easter Orthodox idea of *theosis*, which means a process of "deification", of becoming like God. The word "Christian" means "little Christ." Perhaps to follow Jesus also means being a "little Mary."

George Fox spoke of "answering that of God in everyone,"

blessing others, and allowing "the witness of God in them to bless you." I see this mutual recognition of God Within in Mary's meeting with her cousin Elizabeth: "When Elizabeth heard Mary's greeting, the child leaped in her womb. And Elizabeth was filled with the Holy Spirit and exclaimed with a loud cry, 'Blessed are you among women, and blessed is the fruit of your womb'" (Lk. 1:41–42).

Mary models a combination of inward contemplation and Spirit-led speech. She hears and obeys the leadings of the Spirit. Her "Here am I, the servant of the Lord; let it be with me according to your word" (Lk. 1:38) parallels Jesus' "yet, not my will but yours be done" (Lk. 22:42). It is repeatedly said that she treasures and ponders the prophetic words of others, including her son's, in her heart (Lk. 2:19, 51). In this way she is, in the Quaker phrase, a "humble learner in the school of Christ." As well as treasuring the words of others, she also speaks her own prophetic words. Her intimacy with Spirit leads to God-inspired speech bubbling up within her. Mary's song known as "the Magnificat" (Lk. 1:46–55) is a powerful description of God's promised future, making clear the political nature of God's kingdom.

There are Christmas carols that label Mary as "meek and mild," and Mary can be seen as an entirely passive character who acts merely as a receptacle for God. Because of this, it's important to notice how Mary cooperates with God. She co-conspires with the Spirit to bring God into the world. Mary's virginity has been talked of in damaging anti-sex, sexist ways, but there is another way of looking at it. Her virginity could be seen as a statement of power. Mary is not dependent on a man to get pregnant. Also, the virgin birth is saying that God and humanity together bring about new things that humanity could not achieve by itself. Mary actively contributes her flesh, her humanity to Jesus. Mary not only births Jesus, she is with him throughout his life. She witnesses his ministry, she stands at the foot of the cross when he dies, in solidarity with her crucified son (Jn. 19:25), and we can also assume she's a witness to the Resurrection and the coming of the Holy Spirit at Pentecost. She is both catalyst and witness to the whole Jesus story.

As a Quaker-shaped Christian, I want to be like Mary. I aspire to honor the seed of Christ within myself and others, and birth God into the world. I hope I can faithfully listen to the Spirit speaking to me through the words of others, and speak prophetic words when they are given to me. I want to conspire with God to usher in and embody God's Kingdom, in solidarity with the crucified and ready for the Spirit of Life to rush in and make everything new.

I also need to be cautions. I can never fully identify with Mary. She's a teenage, brown, Jewish refugee girl from the middle east, which I am not. I need to accept her difference from me and be challenged by it. The metaphor of pregnancy won't work for everyone, especially those who have had difficult or tragic pregnancies, or people who long for pregnancies that won't come. I can't experience pregnancy and I don't want to ignorantly romanticize it. Mary remains a character who both inspires me with her faith, and confronts me with her difference, challenging me to remain open to the wild Spirit of Love that blows where it will.

In this book I have offered my own personal Quaker-shaped Christianity. In a faith community where people use different religious language, a key question is: how do we talk to one another? I hope I have modeled one way of answering that question. In sharing how the Jesus story makes sense of life for me, I hope to hear what stories make sense of life for others. Only when we share our deepest held truths can we be fully in community with one another. Quakers often say that underneath our different words, we are all talking about the same thing. One of the risks we take when we share our stories with one another, is that we will find this is not actually true. We might find fundamental disagreement. Where is the common ground between myself and someone who does not believe in a transcendent God, or someone who believes the Bible to be irrelevant? Insisting our beliefs don't matter, or that we should abandon words and retreat into silence, won't help us live a fuller common life.

Maybe the seed could be a meeting place, a shared story for Quakers of different theological languages. Together we could speak about the good seed within us. We nurture this seed in community, opening ourselves to the light that will enable it to grow in ourselves and in others. We can help each other to protect the seed from those forces that work against abundant life, against human flourishing. This inner and outer work is hard, so hard that the seed has to be broken open, to die, in order to grow. The seed is small as a grain of mustard, but it has within it the power to become a huge Tree of Life. We don't know exactly what this Tree will look like. We just know that it will be good.

Author Biography

Mark Russ is a writer, theologian and teacher, who works for Woodbrooke, the international Quaker learning and research organization based in Britain. Since 2013 Mark has written useful, Quaker-shaped Christian theology on his blog jollyquaker.com. His theological interests include hope, whiteness, the roots of modern Quaker thought and the theology of Jürgen Moltmann. Before retraining as a theologian, Mark enjoyed a successful decade as a music teacher in London, and spent a year visiting and living in various faith-based intentional communities in the UK and USA. He holds an MA in Systematic and Philosophical Theology from the University of Nottingham. He lives with his husband in Birmingham, England.

Note to reader

Thank you for purchasing *Quaker Shaped Christianity*. I hope you have found it useful, thought provoking, and even inspiring. If you have a few moments, please feel free to add your review of the book at your favorite online site for feedback. Also, if you would like to engage further with my theological thought, please visit my website for an ever expanding range of blog posts, and news on upcoming work: https://jollyquaker.com/

In gratitude and friendship, Mark Russ

Notes

I take a "patchwork" approach to my religious life, and "patchwork" is a particularly apt description of this book. My Quaker-shaped Christianity is a sewing together of a variety of theological materials created by other people. If the preceding chapters of this book are the front of a tapestry, this section is where I turn the tapestry around and show you all the different threads on the back. This book is dedicated to my theological mentors, and I want to honor all the people whose voices have shaped this book by naming them here. This section is also for readers who want to explore the ideas in this book further, and perhaps come to different conclusions than I have. I have named those authors whose thoughts I explicitly draw upon in this book. There are many other thinkers who have influenced me more generally, and I can only apologize for not being able to name them all here.

The epigraph comes from the preface of Jürgen Moltmann's *The Coming of God: Christian Eschatology* (1996).

Scripture quotations are from *New Revised Standard Version Bible: Anglicized Edition*, copyright © 1989, 1995 National Council of the Churches of Christ in the United States of America. Used by permission. All rights reserved worldwide.

Introduction: My Quaker-shaped Christianity

The idea that Quakers find unity in a shared silence is further explained in Pink Dandelion's *An Introduction to Quakerism* (2007). The image of Jesus as the key that fits the lock comes from G. K. Chesterton's *Orthodoxy: A Personal Philosophy*, (1908).

Chapter 1 The Jesus Story – Approaching the Bible

In describing "the Quest for the Historical Jesus" I have been guided by James Carleton Paget and Francis Watson's chapters in *The Cambridge Companion to Jesus*, edited by Markus N. A. Bockmuehl (2001). The idea that searching for the Historical Jesus is like looking into a deep well comes from George Tyrrell's *Christianity at the Crossroads* (1909). I am indebted to Kathryn Tanner's *Theories of Culture: A New Agenda for Theology* (1997) for the description of Christianity a community of argument. I have found both Willie James Jennings' *The Christian Imagination* (2010) and Bruce D. Marshall's chapter in *The Cambridge Companion to Christian Doctrine* (1997) helpful in understanding Jesus the Jew, particularly Jennings' prompt to consider what it means to be a Gentile. Julian of Norwich's description of Jesus as Mother can be found in her *Showings*, translated by Edmund Colledge and James Walsh (1978). Books that I have found useful regarding gender and the Bible include *Sisters in the Wilderness* (1993) by Delores S. Williams, and *Womanist Midrash* (2017) by Wilda Gafney. When I write of inhabiting the Jesus story I am deeply influenced by "narrative theology," particularly as found in George A. Lindbeck's *The Nature of Doctrine: Religion and Theology in a Postliberal Age,* (1984), Stanley Hauerwas' *The Peaceable Kingdom: A Primer in Christian Ethics* (1983), and Gerard Loughlin's *Telling God's Story: Bible, Church, and Narrative Theology* (1996).

Chapter 2 Why Only One Story? – Christianity and Universalism

For an example of how Quakers use the phrase "rooted in Christianity, open to new light," see Timothy Ashworth and Alex Wildwood's *Rooted in Christianity, Open to New Light: Quaker Spiritual Diversity* (2009). My critique of universalism draws on Gavin D'Costa's *The Meeting of Religions and the Trinity* (2000), Chapter 13 of Daniel L. Migliore's *Faith Seeking Understanding: An Introduction to Christian Theology* (2014), and Lindbeck's *The Nature of Doctrine*. The relationship of universalism to colonialism comes from Jennings' *The Christian Imagination*. My comments

on right belief and right action are informed by my reading of
Black Theology, particularly Anthony G. Reddie's *Theologizing
Brexit* (2019). I was introduced to the idea of God as a God of
broad places through the work of Jürgen Moltmann, for whom
this is a central theme. See, for example, his autobiography *A
Broad Place* (2007). The quote from Robert Barclay can be found
in paragraph 27.05 of Britain Yearly Meeting's *Quaker Faith and
Practice* (1995).

Chapter 3 A Christ-shaped Future

My approach of starting at the end of the story and working
backwards is informed chiefly by Jürgen Moltmann's *Theology of
Hope* (1967), but also by Frank Kermode's *The Sense of an Ending*
(1967). For a more detailed background to this way of thinking,
see my article "Quaker Eschatology in Britain through the Lens
of Narrative" in *Quaker Studies* 25, no. 2 (2020): 207–25.

For more information on fundamentalist approaches to the
end of the world, see *The Continuum History of Apocalypticism*
(2003), edited by McGinn, Collins, and Stein, and Robert G.
Clouse's chapter on "Fundamentalist Theology" in *The Oxford
Handbook of Eschatology* (2010). For a very readable introduction
to these issues, see Michael J. Gorman's *Reading Revelation
Responsibly* (2011).

My understanding of God's arrival is shaped by Moltmann's
work in general, and specifically by his *The Coming of God*. My
understanding of the early Quaker approach to God's arrival
comes from Douglas Gwyn's *Apocalypse of the Word: The Life and
Message of George Fox* (1986) and *Heaven on Earth: Quakers and
the Second Coming* by "Ben" Pink Dandelion, Douglas Gwyn,
and Timothy Peat (1998). The quote from Elizabeth Bathurst
can be found in her "Truth's vindication," printed in *Hidden
in Plain Sight: Quaker Women's Writings, 1650–1700*, edited by
Garman, Applegate, Benefiel, Meredith (1996). James Nayler's
words on the eternal sabbath are from "To All the World's

Professors" found at http://www.qhpress.org/texts/nayler/ toall.html. Nayler's apocalyptic warning is from "A Salutation to the Seed Of God" (1655) which can be found at http:// www.qhpress.org/texts/nayler/sal_seed.html. My thoughts on Quakers and the Sabbath are inspired by Moltmann's *God in Creation: An Ecological Doctrine of Creation* (1985).

Chapter 4 Resurrection

I discovered the significance of Jesus' post-Resurrection encounter with Peter in Rowan Williams' *Resurrection: Interpreting the Easter Gospel* (1982). My thinking on the relationship of the Resurrection to our bodies is influenced by Jürgen Moltmann's *God in Creation* and Nancey C. Murphy's *Bodies and Souls, or Spirited Bodies?* (2006). The idea that the Resurrection is not a historical event, in terms of cause and effect, is from Moltmann's *Theology of Hope*.

Chapter 5 Crucifixion

A helpful introduction to the theology of sin can be found in Darlene Fozard Weaver's chapter in the *T&T Clark Handbook of Theological Anthropology*, edited by Mary Ann Hinsdale and Stephen Okey (2021). I have been greatly influenced by the idea of the "banality of evil," a phrase coined in Hannah Arendt's *Eichmann in Jerusalem: A Report on the Banality of Evil* (1963). John Woolman's words on the "seeds of war" are from his tract *A Word of Remembrance and Caution to the Rich* and are quoted in paragraph 23.16 of *Quaker Faith & Practice: The Book of Christian Discipline of the Yearly Meeting of the Religious Society of Friends (Quakers) in Britain* (2013). The idea of being saints and sinners comes from a famous saying of Martin Luther, which in Latin reads *"simul justus et peccator."*

My thinking on the cross has been profoundly shaped by James H. Cone's *The cross and the Lynching Tree* (2011) and Jürgen Moltmann's *The Crucified God* (1974), two of the most important books I've ever read. I was introduced to the idea of the Crucifixion scene being an image of the church by Wyatt Houtz's post on his blog *The PostBarthian*, "Karl Barth on Good Friday: The Criminals Crucified with Jesus Formed the First Christian Community," (April 18, 2019). https://postbarthian. com/2019/04/17 Moltmann /karl-barth-on-good-friday-the-criminals-crucified-with-jesus-formed-the-first-christian-community/.

Chapter 6. Planting a Seed

Isaac Penington's (1616–1679) "The Seed of God and of His Kingdom" can be found at http://www.qhpress.org/texts/penington/seed.html, and his much loved words about sinking down to the seed come from "Some Directions to the Panting Soul" (1661), found at http://www.qhpress.org/texts/penington/panting.html. Margaret Fell's "Women's Speaking Justified" can be found at http://www.qhpress.org/texts/fell.html. George Fox's vision of the earthquake comes from his *Journal*, edited by John L. Nickalls (1952). Nayler's words are from "A Salutation to the Seed Of God". Robert Barclay's thoughts on the seed come from *An Apology for the True Christian Divinity* (1678), which can be found at http://www.qhpress.org/texts/barclay/apology/. Elizabeth Bathurst is quoted from her "Truth's vindication." I have also been helped by many of the chapters in *Early Quakers and Their Theological Thought*, edited by Angell and Dandelion (2015).

I first encountered the idea of Christians spiritually emulating Mary and birthing Christ into the world in the work of tenth-century theologian Symeon the New Theologian, in the book *On The Mystical Life: The Ethical Discourses* (1995). George Fox's words on "answering that of God in everyone" are from his *Journal*.

CHRISTIAN ALTERNATIVE
BOOKS

THE NEW OPEN SPACES

Throughout the two thousand years of Christian tradition there
have been, and still are, groups and individuals that exist in
the margins and upon the edge of faith. But in Christianity's
contrapuntal history it has often been these outcasts and
pioneers that have forged contemporary orthodoxy out
of former radicalism as belief evolves to engage with and
encompass the ever-changing social and scientific realities. Real
faith lies not in the comfortable certainties of the Orthodox,
but somewhere in a half-glimpsed hinterland on the dirt track
to Emmaus, where the Death of God meets the Resurrection,
where the supernatural Christ meets the historical Jesus,
and where the revolution liberates both the oppressed and
the oppressors.
Welcome to Christian Alternative... a space at the edge where
the light shines through.
If you have enjoyed this book, why not tell other readers by
posting a review on your preferred book site.

Recent bestsellers from Christian Alternative are:

Bread Not Stones
The Autobiography of An Eventful Life
Una Kroll
The spiritual autobiography of a truly remarkable woman
and a history of the struggle for ordination in the Church of
England.
Paperback: 978-1-78279-804-0 ebook: 978-1-78279-805-7

The Quaker Way
A Rediscovery
Rex Ambler
Although fairly well known, Quakerism is not well understood.
The purpose of this book is to explain how Quakerism works as
a spiritual practice.
Paperback: 978-1-78099-657-8 ebook: 978-1-78099-658-5

Blue Sky God
The Evolution of Science and Christianity
Don MacGregor
Quantum consciousness, morphic fields and blue-sky
thinking about God and Jesus the Christ.
Paperback: 978-1-84694-937-1 ebook: 978-1-84694-938-8

Celtic Wheel of the Year
Tess Ward
An original and inspiring selection of prayers combining
Christian and Celtic Pagan traditions, and interweaving their
calendars into a single pattern of prayer for every morning
and night of the year.
Paperback: 978-1-90504-795-6

Readers of ebooks can buy or view any of these bestsellers by clicking on the live link in the title. Most titles are published in paperback and as an ebook. Paperbacks are available in traditional bookshops. Both print and ebook formats are available online.

Find more titles and sign up to our readers' newsletter at
http://www.johnhuntpublishing.com/christianity
Follow us on Facebook at
https://www.facebook.com/ChristianAlternative